# Conne(

## A Catholic Small Group Discussion Guide for Lent Year B

### The Evangelical Catholic
#### Lectionary Bible Study Series

723 State Street
Madison Wisconsin 53703
www.evangelicalcatholic.org

1st Printing February 2009

2nd Printing December 2011

Copyright 2009 The Evangelical Catholic

All Rights Reserved

Printed in the USA

Revised Standard Version of the Bible Catholic Edition, copyright 1965, 1966 by the Division of Christian Education of the National Council of the Churches of Christ in the United States of America. Used by permission. All rights reserved.

Excerpts from the English translation of the *Catechism of the Catholic Church* for use in the United States of America Copyright 1994, United States Catholic Conference, Inc. – *Liberia Editrice Vaticana*.

# Table of Contents

Introduction . . . . . . . . . . . . . . . . . . . . . . . . . . . . . . . . 1

A Time for Faith: 1st Sunday . . . . . . . . . . . . . . . . . . . . . . . 5

A Time to Listen: 2nd Sunday . . . . . . . . . . . . . . . . . . . . . . 15

A Time for Action: 3rd Sunday . . . . . . . . . . . . . . . . . . . . . . 25

A Time to Return to the Light: 4th Sunday. . . . . . . . . . . . . . . . 35

A Time to Die: 5th Sunday . . . . . . . . . . . . . . . . . . . . . . . . 45

A Time to Weep: Palm Sunday of the Lord's Passion . . . . . . . . . . . 55

A Time to Truly Live: Easter Sunday . . . . . . . . . . . . . . . . . . . 69

Appendix A: A Guide to *Lectio Divina* . . . . . . . . . . . . . . . . . 83

Appendix B: Learning to Listen to God . . . . . . . . . . . . . . . . . 87

Appendix C: Saint Ignatius and the Two Standards. . . . . . . . . . . . 93

Small Group Discussion Guidelines . . . . . . . . . . . . . . . . . . . . 97

The Role of a Facilitator . . . . . . . . . . . . . . . . . . . . . . . . 101

Materials to Have at Your Small Group . . . . . . . . . . . . . . . . . 107

A Guide to the Sacrament of Reconciliation . . . . . . . . . . . . . . 109

An Examination of Conscience . . . . . . . . . . . . . . . . . . . . . 111

# TIME TO BEGIN

## Introduction

*"Now is the acceptable time; behold, now is the day of salvation."*

*2 Corinthians 6:2*

How much of life we put off!

> "I'll organize that closet some day…"

> "Tomorrow I'll start a diet…"

> "I'll quit smoking once I'm past this stressful time."

> "I'll repair that _____ at home when work isn't so busy …"

How many people do you know who never quit smoking, never lose weight, never fix things long broken and unattended?

Isn't this true of everyone? We all put off what we know would be better to do.

And don't we do the same thing with God?

> I'll pray regularly once the kids are in school, once they're at college, once they're grown up…

> I'll make a confession another time…

> When I'm not so tired from work, I'll make time to read the Scriptures…

As important as the physical parts of life are - health, order, home - if what we say we believe about God is true, how much more important are our supernatural lives! Our very hearts and souls are too often what is broken and unattended, in need of repair only God can provide. Yet we do not go to the only one who can help us.

If God is love, how can we hope that what comes from love will be part of our lives if we aren't growing in our relationship to him? Without God/love, how can we hope to be kind, generous and forgiving of ourselves and others? How can God help us to grow beyond putting on airs, being rude, self-seeking or prone to anger? How can we ever bear with one another, overcome pride, become patient? In the great hymn to love St. Paul wrote in his first letter to the Corinthians, he even attributes hope to love, and how can we live without hope? (1 Cor 13:1-13)

If God really so loved the world that he sent His only son, Jesus, to save us, then don't we want to deeply appreciate what that means, what that cost, understand not just in our heads, but in our hearts?

For it is the movement of our hearts God seeks at Lent: "Rend your hearts, not your garments and return to the LORD," exhorts the prophet Joel.

"Now is the acceptable time. Now is the moment of salvation," says St. Paul.

The Church uses these readings every Ash Wednesday to remind us, because we need to be reminded to tend what is too often neglected. We are human beings. The demands of the physical world will always seem more pressing than those of the supernatural. We must have this season to prompt us to put God, prayer, Scripture and the sacraments at the top of our "To Do" lists. We need encouragement to truly "rend our hearts," not just give up chocolate or television.

*Connection to the Cross* seeks to help us do this. Through reflecting on the Sunday readings, praying together, and encouraging one another to daily prayer, we hope to love Jesus more dearly and follow him more nearly, follow him even to the cross.

As Christians we believe we come to God through Christ. The light came into the world: without him, we are in darkness. It is through him that we see things as they really are instead of being duped by the lies of the Evil One, whom Jesus called "the Father of lies." (John

8:44) Reflecting together in the light of the words and actions of Jesus, and those of his earliest followers, we can experience the truth he proclaimed: God's kingdom is indeed "at hand." (Mark 1:15) It is so close we can literally taste it in Eucharist because of what Christ did for us.

Lent has the power to bring forth a great harvest in our lives and our churches. Seeds are planted in our hearts through prayer, especially praying over the Scriptures that help us know Christ, and God in him. *Connection to the Cross* will plant these seeds. Groups should meet before the first Sunday of Lent, and weekly after that, so you can read and pray over the Sunday readings before you hear them at Mass. Our intention is that groups do not meet during Holy Week. They might consider taking part in the Triduum as a group. The last study, Week 7, is meant to be read in a final meeting after Easter Sunday.

Attend meetings, and the seeds will be scattered in your life. It's up to each one of us to water them by following the recommendations for the coming week. Fasting and almsgiving, the other two Lenten observations, will fertilize these seeds as nothing else can. When Holy week comes, allowing the field to be drenched in the blood of the Lamb and warmed by the resurrection of the Son on Easter will bring forth fruit in our lives -- twenty, thirty, even a hundred fold.

Now is the acceptable time. Now is the moment of salvation. Don't miss it!

# A TIME FOR FAITH

## 1st Sunday of Lent

*"The Spirit immediately drove him out into the wilderness."*

*Mark 1:12*

*A Time for Faith*

## Opening Prayer

**Slowly read the following prayer aloud together.**

In the name of the Father, and of the Son, and of the Holy Spirit:

O Lord and Master of our lives,
keep from us the spirit of indifference
and discouragement,
lust of power
and idle chatter.

Instead, grant to us, your servants,
the spirit of wholeness of being,
humble-mindedness, patience, and love.

O Lord and King, grant us the grace
to be aware of our sins
and not to judge our brothers and sisters;
for you are blessed now and ever and forever.

Amen.[1]

---

[1] Based on the ancient Lenten Prayer of St. Ephrem the Syrian, an especially important prayer during Lent for Christians in the East.

# 1st Sunday of Lent

## Introduction

**Have someone read the following aloud.**

This week, at the very beginning of Lent, the readings show us important characteristics about God. God will challenge us in new ways this Lent, if our picture of God is rooted in truth rather than misconceptions. The Church gives us these readings at the beginning of the journey to remind us of God's goodness and deepen our trust in our Father.

1. Have you had particularly positive or negative experiences with coaches or teachers? How did the attributes of the teacher or coach affect your ability to embrace their challenges?

## Scripture and Tradition

### Reading: Genesis 9:8-15

**Have someone read the following passage aloud.**

⁸Then God said to Noah and to his sons with him, ⁹"Behold, I establish my covenant with you and your descendants after you, ¹⁰and with every living creature that is with you, the birds, the cattle, and every beast of the earth with you, as many as came out of the ark. ¹¹I establish my covenant with you, that never again shall all flesh be cut off by the waters of a flood, and never again shall there be a flood to destroy the earth." ¹²And God said, "This is the sign of the covenant which I make between me and you and every living creature that is with you, for all

future generations: ¹³I set my bow in the cloud, and it shall be a sign of the covenant between me and the earth. ¹⁴When I bring clouds over the earth and the bow is seen in the clouds, ¹⁵I will remember my covenant which is between me and you and every living creature of all flesh; and the waters shall never again become a flood to destroy all flesh.

2. What is the covenant that God makes with Noah and his descendants?

3. How do you think Noah and his family felt about this covenant?

4. Noah and his family didn't have the written Scriptures or the *Catechism* to teach them about God; they learned who God was by the things he said and did.

   - What do you think they thought God was like when he told them to build the ark? What attributes might they have used to describe God, given this command?

   - How do you think they would have described God when he flooded the world?

   - When he gave them this new covenant, how might it have changed their view of this God that they were coming to know?

5. What does it say about this God that he gave them a sign in the sky of this covenant?

# Reading: 1 Peter 3:18-22

**Have someone read the following aloud.**

¹⁸For Christ also died for sins once for all, the righteous for the unrighteous, that he might bring us to God, being put to death in the flesh but made alive in the spirit; ¹⁹in which he went and preached to the spirits in prison, ²⁰who formerly did not obey, when God's patience

## 1st Sunday of Lent

waited in the days of Noah, during the building of the ark, in which a few, that is, eight persons, were saved through water. [21]Baptism, which corresponds to this, now saves you, not as a removal of dirt from the body but as an appeal to God for a clear conscience, through the resurrection of Jesus Christ, [22]who has gone into heaven and is at the right hand of God, with angels, authorities, and powers subject to him.

6. What does this passage tell us about the attributes of God?

7. Christ's mission on earth was to reveal God to us. What can we see about God through the qualities of Christ highlighted in this passage?

8. What does the end of verse 18 through verse 20 say that Christ did? What do you think this is talking about? Where is this prison? What can we see about God from these actions?

## Reading: Mark 1:12-15

**Have someone read the following aloud.**

[12]The Spirit immediately drove him out into the wilderness. [13]And he was in the wilderness forty days, tempted by Satan; and he was with the wild beasts; and the angels ministered to him. [14]Now after John was arrested, Jesus came into Galilee, preaching the gospel of God, [15]and saying, "The time is fulfilled, and the kingdom of God is at hand; repent, and believe in the gospel."

9. Why does the text say Jesus went to the wilderness?

10. Why do you think God wanted Jesus to go into the wilderness?

11. The gospel writer mentions several aspects of Jesus' experience in the desert. We might already know that there is a longer, very rich story behind Mark's brief mention of Satanic temptations. But why the wild beasts? Why the angels?

12. What does Jesus do after his time in the wilderness is over?

13. What do you think he meant by his words in v.15? How can we understand this teaching today?

14. Lent is 40 days (excluding Sundays). Because God wants all of us to go into the wilderness as Jesus did, the Church gives this privileged time each year to encourage us. What will it mean for you to go into the wilderness this holy season?

15. What attributes of God that we discussed earlier are the most encouraging as you set out for the wilderness this Lent?

16. How do you think Satan will tempt you? What are the wild beasts for you? Have you ever felt angels attending you through people, prayer, etc.?

## Connection to the Cross This Week

- Spend time praying with the daily readings this week. They are chosen very intentionally in order to lead you deeper into conversion. You will find them listed below and at the end of every chapter. Appendix A describes *Lectio Divina*, a method from the ancient Church on how to read and meditate on Scripture prayerfully. This practice will enrich your Lenten experience and your whole life.

- You might write St. Ephrem's prayer on a note card and tape it to your bathroom mirror or your car dashboard. This will help you pray it everyday this week to remind you of your spiritual goals this Lent.

- Take 20 minutes of quiet time and meditate on what means Satan might use to tempt you away from your Lenten practices. He is not that original. Temptations usually come in the form of his same old lies and tricks. He only finds new ones when

## 1st Sunday of Lent

he sees you have become impervious to the old. What are your "wild beasts?" Make concrete plans for how you might resist your habitual temptations. Many spiritual teachers suggest planning distractions. What exactly will you do to distract yourself when temptation comes?

- Go to a daily Mass this week at a local parish if you don't normally attend. Make it something of a journey away from the busyness of your day and into the wilderness in order to find God.

**This Week's Readings**

Monday - Lev 19:1-2, 11-18;  Ps 20:8, 9, 10, 15; Matt 25:31-46
Tuesday - Isa 55:10-11; Ps 34:4-5, 6-7, 16-17, 18-19; Matt 6:7-15
Wednesday - Jonah 3:1-10; Ps 51:3-4, 12-13, 18-19; Luke 11:29-32
Thursday - Esth C:12, 14-16, 23-25; Ps 138:1-2-3, 7c-8; Matt 7:7-12
Friday - Ezek 18:21-28; Ps 130:1-2, 3-4, 5-8; Matt 5:20-26
Saturday - Deut 26:16-19; Ps 119:1-2, 4-5, 7-8; Matt 5:43-48

## Closing Prayer

Spend a little time praying for each other at the beginning of this Lent. The facilitator could ask for any prayer petitions that people have. The group could then spend time sharing their personal needs with each other and perhaps everyone could offer a simple prayer for the person on the right. When the group finishes praying for one another, pray the Closing Prayer aloud together.

As always with prayer, just be natural, and don't worry about what you will say. Jesus told us the Holy Spirit would give us the words we need. Eloquence is far less important than a prayerful spirit.

# A Time for Faith

*Here is an example for how this might sound:*

[Jim]: I would like prayer for my friend…

[Sue - Person to Jim's right]: In the name of the Father, and of the Son, and of the Holy Spirit: Lord, I pray that you would help Jim's friend with…Amen.

[Sue]: I would like prayer for my work…

[Laura] – Person to Sue's right]: In the name of the Father, and of the Son, and of the Holy Spirit: Jesus, please help Sue at work…Amen.

**After last person prays, all pray the following together.**

O Christ Jesus,
when all is darkness
and we feel our weakness and helplessness,
give us the sense of your presence,
your love, and your strength.
Help us to have perfect trust
in your protecting love
and strengthening power,
so that nothing may frighten or worry us,
for, living close to you,
we shall see your hand,
your purpose, your will through all things.

Amen.

**St. Ignatius of Loyola, (1491-1556)**

# Notes

# A TIME TO LISTEN

## 2nd Sunday of Lent

*"Then a cloud overshadowed them, and from the cloud there came a voice, 'This is my Son, the Beloved; listen to him!'"*

*Mark 9:7*

# A Time to Listen

## Opening Prayer

**Have someone read the following prayer aloud.**

In the name of the Father, and of the Son,
and of the Holy Spirit:

Jesus,
You ask us to go with you

up the mountain.
At the top
we stumble

on our words
look for something to do.

Teach us Father
how to be still
to listen
to your Son.
Make our hearts still now,
open them to hear
and receive

your word—
The Word of Life.
Amen

## 2nd Sunday of Lent

## Introduction

1. On a scale of 1-10, rate your comfort level with silence with people you know, and then with people you do not know.

   (1 being "I can't stand it." 10 being "I am completely at ease.")

2. On a scale of 1-10, rate your comfort level with silence when you are alone.

   (1 being "I can't stand it." 10 being "I am completely at ease.")

3. Do you prefer being silent when you're alone or in the company of others?

4. Do you ever spend silent time with God?

5. If yes, on a scale of 1-10, rate your comfort level with silence with God in prayer.

## Scripture and Tradition

**Have someone read the following aloud to the group.**

Last week we examined some of the great attributes of God and his faithfulness to lead us patiently into goodness. In this week's Gospel, Jesus leads Peter, James, and John up the mountain to be with him, the Father, and the Holy Spirit.

*A Time to Listen*

# Reading: Mark 9:2-10

**Have someone read the following passage aloud.**

² Six days later, Jesus took with him Peter and James and John, and led them up a high mountain apart, by themselves. And he was transfigured before them, ³and his clothes became dazzling white, such as no one on earth could bleach them. ⁴And there appeared to them Elijah with Moses, who were talking with Jesus. ⁵Then Peter said to Jesus, "Rabbi, it is good for us to be here; let us make three dwellings, one for you, one for Moses, and one for Elijah." ⁶He did not know what to say, for they were terrified. ⁷Then a cloud overshadowed them, and from the cloud there came a voice, "This is my Son, the Beloved; listen to him!" ⁸Suddenly when they looked around, they saw no one with them any more, but only Jesus.

⁹As they were coming down the mountain, he ordered them to tell no one about what they had seen, until after the Son of Man had risen from the dead. ¹⁰So they kept the matter to themselves, questioning what this rising from the dead could mean.

6. **What strikes you from this story? Is there anything you hadn't noticed previously?**

7. **Peter, James and John see that Jesus is in conversation with Moses and Elijah. Recap the series of their responses and other events in the order in which they occur in this story.**

8. **What do you make of Peter offering to build dwellings for the three of them?**

9. **Do you know people whose primary way of responding to God is to serve through labor? Are you such a person? What is comfortable about this kind of service?**

10. **What do you think the apostles fear?**

## 2nd Sunday of Lent

11. **Biblical interpreters tell us Moses represents the law and Elijah the prophets.** (See *Catechism of the Catholic Church*, paragraph 555 for more information.) How does understanding Moses' and Elijah's roles expand your understanding of what is happening in this scene?

12. The same *Catechism* paragraph tells us that the entire Trinity is present on Mount Tabor for the Transfiguration. How would you identify the presence of the Holy Spirit?[2]

13. What do you think is the significance of God's command to the disciples: "This is my Son, the Beloved; listen to him!" What does it mean to listen to Christ? How do you do this?

14. Think about your most powerful experience of God. What was the setting? Was it in the course of daily life? Were you in prayer? How did it affect you? How did you respond? What did you take away from it? If you would like, please share with the group.

15. Jesus wants all of us to come away from the crowd to be with him in a quiet place. What hindrances do we face to following him up the mountain? What stops us from going?

16. What obstacles do we face once there? Have you experienced any that the disciples experienced on the mountain top? Fear? Compulsion to speak? To act? Do you know how just to be in the presence of God? What are some concrete things you could do to overcome these obstacles?

## Reading

**Have someone read the following aloud to the group.**

> Jesus in His Divinity is the source of contemplation. When the presence of the Divine is experienced as overwhelming, we are inwardly compelled to contemplate. Such was the situation of the apostles on Mount Tabor when they witnessed the glory of God shining through the humanity of Jesus. They fell on their faces…

---

[2] After discussing this, feel free to have a print-out of the *Catechism* paragraph ready for the group to read together. Share reactions to the paragraph.

## A Time to Listen

Jesus took with him the three disciples who were best prepared to receive the grace of contemplation; that is, the ones who had made the most headway in changing their hearts. God approached them through their sense by means of the vision on the mountain. At first they were overawed and delighted. Peter wanted to remain there forever. Suddenly a cloud covered them, hiding the vision and leaving their senses empty and quiet, yet attentive and alert. The gesture of falling on their faces accurately expressed their state of mind. It was a posture of adoration, gratitude, and love all rolled into one. The voice from heaven awakened their consciousness to the presence of the Spirit, who had always been speaking within them, but whom until then they had never been able to hear. Their interior emptiness was filled with the luminous presence of the divine. At Jesus' touch they returned to their ordinary perceptions and saw him as he was before but with the transformed consciousness of faith. They no longer saw him as a mere human being. Their receptive and active faculties had been unified by the Spirit; the interior and exterior word of God had become one. For those who have attained this consciousness, daily life is a continual and increasing revelation of God. The words they hear in scripture and in the liturgy confirm what they have learned through the prayer that is contemplation.

Thomas Keating, O.C.S.O.
*Open Mind, Open Heart,* pp. 16-18

17. Keating says that Jesus took the three disciples because they had made the most headway in changing their hearts to receive grace. Does it make sense to you that we have to be prepared in order to be with Jesus and experience God in prayer? Do you think this means that we have to "earn" or "merit" our way into being with Jesus/experiencing God?

18. Keating ignores the reference to the apostles' fear, instead seeing delight. Do you think this is a legitimate reading?

19. Keating refers to Jesus touching the apostles. He does this in Matthew's version of the transfiguration, telling them not to fear. How does that change your experience of this story?

## Connection to the Cross This Week

- In your daily prayer, give some time to sitting quietly in God's presence. If you are able, attend daily Mass this week. Afterwards spend time sitting in silence in front of the tabernacle. If distractions come, it's okay, just refocus yourself. Many techniques can help us sit comfortably in silent prayer. One easy one is to picture your heart as an empty bowl, tilted out toward God, being wordlessly filled by God.

  **Sometime this week try the following exercise:**

  First, sit quietly a few moments to relax.
  Think about what keeps you from being silent with God. Worries? Preoccupations? Negative thoughts? Fear? Too much to do? Guilt?
  Try to identify the hindrances.
  In your mind, approach Jesus on the cross. Give your hindrances to him. Hang them or lay them at the foot of the cross. Ask Jesus to carry the burden of them for you. Then sit quietly at the foot of the cross. If you are weary, rest your head on the rough wood. Touch his foot. Remember it is for love of you that he is hanging there, dying.
  Rest in that love.
  Try to do this exercise each day this week. The things that keep you from silence will most likely keep coming up. Just remember it is normal and growth in this kind of prayer takes time. But it is worth it! Peace is the sweetest fruit that comes from this type of prayer. Persevere, and it will be yours.

## A Time to Listen

- For more help with silence in prayer and distractions, see Appendix B. This quick read offers advice from the great teachers of prayer in our tradition, from St. Teresa of Avila to Thomas Keating. These wise men and women have left us a treasure trove. Take advantage of this condensed version!

**This Week's Readings**

Monday -  Dan 9:4b-10; Ps 78:8, 9, 11+13; Luke 6:36-38
Tuesday -  Isa 1:10, 16-20; Ps 50:8-9, 16bc-17, 21+23; Matt 23:1-12
Wednesday -  Jer 18:18-20; Ps 31:5-6, 14, 15-16; Matt 20:17-28
Thursday -  Jer 17:5-10; Ps 1:1-2, 3, 4+6; Luke 16:19-31
Friday -  Gen 37:3-4, 12-13a, 17b-28a; Ps 105:16-17, 18-19, 20-21; Matt 21:33-43, 45-46
Saturday -  Mic 7:14-15, 18-20; Ps 103:1-2, 3-4, 9-10, 11-12; Luke 15:1-3, 11-32

## Closing Prayer

**Please have someone who reads well proclaim this passage slowly and thoughtfully, allowing pauses for consideration as appropriate.**

In the name of the Father, of the Son, and of the Holy Spirit:

## 2nd Sunday of Lent

Into the silence.
An invitation
to the sad places
the dark places
the places we keep hidden.
Buried under
Noise
Activity
Preoccupation,
there is the quiet place
where God waits.
One foot
now another
descend the stair.
Now,
there,

in your heart
breathe
the Spirit
who isn't afraid
of your sin
of your weakness
of your shame
but who waits
in the very stuff of it
to embrace you
to comfort you
to burn away
what keeps you apart.

Amen.

# Notes

# THE TIME FOR ACTION

## 3rd Sunday of Lent

*"'Zeal for your house will consume me.'"*

*John 2:17*

*A Time for Action*

## Opening Prayer

Have someone read the following prayer aloud. You could also have a different person read each paragraph.

**Prayer for Guidance**

In the name of the Father, and of the Son,
and of the Holy Spirit:

O creator past all telling,
you have appointed from the treasures of your wisdom
the hierarchies of angels,
disposing them in wondrous order
above the bright heavens,
and have so beautifully set out all parts of the universe.

You we call the true fount of wisdom
and the noble origin of all things.
Be pleased to shed
on the darkness of mind in which I was born,
The twofold beam of your light
and warmth to dispel my ignorance and sin.

You make eloquent the tongues of children.
Then instruct my speech
and touch my lips with graciousness.
Make me keen to understand, quick to learn,
able to remember;
make me delicate to interpret and ready to speak.

Guide my going in and going forward,
lead home my going forth.
You are true God and true man,
and live for ever and ever.

*St. Thomas Aquinas, 1225-74*

*3rd Sunday of Lent*

## Introduction

Choose one of the following to discuss.

1. Was there ever a time when you felt you had to take a public stand for what you thought was right? What was difficult about this? Were there positive or negative consequences?

2. Was there ever a time when you wanted to take a public stand for what you thought was right, but didn't? What were the consequences of that decision to remain silent?

3. Have you ever seen someone else take such a public stand? What was your impression, response to that person at the time?

## Scripture and Tradition

**Have someone read the following aloud.**

In the first week of Lent, Jesus went off by himself to be with God at the prompting of the Holy Spirit. Much later in his ministry, but always read at the second Sunday of Lent, Jesus took three future leaders of the Church off to be with him in a smaller group. On the mountain top with him they witnessed a theophany: God revealing himself in the person of Jesus, and learned that they must listen to Jesus as they have never listened before.

On the third Sunday of Lent, the time for prayer, silence, learning, listening is past. Jesus takes action. Jesus teaches us that prayer and profound connection with God the Father should underlie every action, but that sometimes, we must act.

## *A Time for Action*

# Reading: John 2:13-25

**Have someone read the following passage aloud.**

[13]The Passover of the Jews was near, and Jesus went up to Jerusalem. [14]In the temple he found people selling cattle, sheep, and doves, and the money-changers seated at their tables. [15]Making a whip of cords, he drove all of them out of the temple, both the sheep and the cattle. He also poured out the coins of the money-changers and overturned their tables. [16]He told those who were selling the doves, "Take these things out of here! Stop making my Father's house a market-place!" [17]His disciples remembered that it was written, "Zeal for your house will consume me." [18]The Jews then said to him, "What sign can you show us for doing this?" [19]Jesus answered them, "Destroy this temple, and in three days I will raise it up." [20]The Jews then said, "This temple has been under construction for forty-six years, and will you raise it up in three days?" [21]But he was speaking of the temple of his body. [22]After he was raised from the dead, his disciples remembered that he had said this; and they believed the scripture and the word that Jesus had spoken.

[23]When he was in Jerusalem during the Passover festival, many believed in his name because they saw the signs that he was doing. [24]But Jesus on his part would not entrust himself to them, because he knew all people [25]and needed no one to testify about anyone; for he himself knew what was in everyone.

> 4. **Has anyone ever seen animals herded with whips? Please describe it for the group.**
>
> If no one has seen herding, try to imagine the temple courtyard, a large open area but still in the midst of a bustling city, filled with animals. It would have been very crowded at Passover. Sacrifice of an animal by each family was part of the temple ritual for Passover. This is why ox and sheep were sold in the temple precinct. (Poorer people brought their own animals from farms, or purchased doves, which were much cheaper.)

5. Describe what such a scene would be like if someone suddenly showed up and started chasing the animals, and possibly the animal merchants, with a whip?

6. Why do you think Jesus runs the animals out of the temple courtyard if they were needed for the religious ritual?

7. Do you think that by driving the animals out, Jesus is protesting against their presence in a sacred place, or was he rejecting animal sacrifice all together, or something else? What were the motivations behind the action he chose to take?

Because the imperial or pagan portraits appeared on most of the currency, Jews commonly could not use it to pay the temple tax necessary to make their sacrifice. The money changers exchanged this unacceptable tender for idol-image-free coinage and took a commission. Like the animal merchants, they provided a service necessary for Jewish rituals.

8. Why do you think John specifically notes that Jesus spilled the money-changers coins?

9. Have you ever witnessed or read about someone acting to disrupt a Church service or religious ceremony out of protest? What was your response?

10. What virtues do you think Jesus embodied while purifying the temple?

11. What virtues would it take for you to act in areas you believe you should? Can you think of ways to cultivate those virtues in your life?

12. What do you think the merchants, money changers, and observers thought when Jesus called the Temple "my Father's house?" (This was not standard terminology.)

## A Time for Action

13. The "Jews"[3] ask Jesus for "a sign authorizing you to do these things." What does this request indicate about their attitude?

14. How does Jesus respond to this request for supernatural credentials?

15. What tone of voice do you think Jesus would have used when he said: "Destroy this temple?" What would that tone indicate to those who heard him?

16. How would you describe a temple? What characterizes a temple?

17. If Jesus is referring to himself when he speaks of the temple, what does this mean for our understanding of ourselves as "the body of Christ?"

# Reading: Exodus 20:1-17

**Have someone read the following passage aloud.**

²⁰Then God spoke all these words:

²I am the Lord your God, who brought you out of the land of Egypt, out of the house of slavery; ³you shall have no other gods before me.

⁴You shall not make for yourself an idol, whether in the form of anything that is in heaven above, or that is on the earth beneath, or that is in the water under the earth. ⁵You shall not bow down to them or worship them; for I the Lord your God am a jealous God, punishing children for the iniquity of parents, to the third and the fourth generation of those who reject me, ⁶but showing steadfast love to the thousandth generation of those who love me and keep my commandments.

⁷You shall not make wrongful use of the name of the Lord your God, for the Lord will not acquit anyone who misuses his name.

---

[3]John uses this term in his gospels to refer to the Jewish leadership, not all Jews. Jesus was a Jew, as was his mother and all first followers. To describe the same scene, the synoptic gospels list the Jewish leadership: "chief priests, scribes and elders." See Matthew 21:27 for an example.

## 3rd Sunday of Lent

⁸Remember the sabbath day, and keep it holy. ⁹For six days you shall labour and do all your work. ¹⁰But the seventh day is a sabbath to the Lord your God; you shall not do any work—you, your son or your daughter, your male or female slave, your livestock, or the alien resident in your towns. ¹¹For in six days the Lord made heaven and earth, the sea, and all that is in them, but rested the seventh day; therefore the Lord blessed the sabbath day and consecrated it.

¹²Honour your father and your mother, so that your days may be long in the land that the Lord your God is giving you.

¹³You shall not murder.

¹⁴You shall not commit adultery.

¹⁵You shall not steal.

¹⁶You shall not bear false witness against your neighbour.

¹⁷You shall not covet your neighbour's house; you shall not covet your neighbour's wife, or male or female slave, or ox, or donkey, or anything that belongs to your neighbour.

18. Why do you think that the Church would couple an Old Testament and a Psalm reading about the law with a gospel where Jesus' actions might have implied, at least to his Jewish observers, that the laws around ritual observance were less important than other aspects of religious practice?

19. What aspects of religious practice does Jesus seem to be elevating above the laws that guide the ritual?

*A Time for Action*

## Connection to the Cross This Week

- Try praying ten minutes a day over some area of your life where you have felt inner stirrings indicating you should or could take action, but haven't. In prayer, seek God's will about this area of your life, and the action that you should take. Use www.Biblegateway.com or another search engine to see if you can find any Scriptures relevant to this issue. Pray faithfully over any you find.

- If you do not have an area of your life where you have felt such stirrings, then this week pray everyday for ten minutes about areas of your life where God does indeed want you to act, even though you have not yet felt any inner impulse to do so. Ask God to reveal to you what action would help you grow as a Christian at this time of your life. Ask God for the courage and strength to act, and the perseverance to follow through with whatever you start under his guidance.

- Lent is a time for prayer, but also one for action. If you have not undertaken a penance or almsgiving, ask Jesus to guide you to this. What penance could you embrace this week out of love for Christ? Perhaps you might skip a meal in order to pray or to spend time with a co-worker who seems lonely. Is there a person or a group who seems to be in need of a gift of money or time? If you feel led to give monetarily, go out of your way to give your contribution in secret. Jesus promises that the Father rewards those who give in secret.

## 3rd Sunday of Lent

### This Week's Readings

Monday - 2 Kgs 5:1-15;, Ps 42:2, 3; 42:3, 4; Luke 4:24-30
Tuesday - Dan 3:25, 34-43; Ps 25:4-5ab, 6+7bc, 8-9; Matt 18:21-35
Wednesday - Deut 4:1, 5-9; Ps 147:12-13, 15-16, 19-20; Matt 5:17-19
Thursday - Jer 7:23-28; Ps 95:1-2, 6-7, 8-9; Luke 11:14-23
Friday - Hos 14:2-10; Ps 81:6c-8a, 8bc-9, 10-11ab, 14+17; Mark 12:28b-34
Saturday - Hos 6:1-6; Ps 51:3-4, 18-19, 20-21ab; Luke 18:9-14

## Closing Prayer

Perhaps you want to share your needs with each other and spend time praying for them. Afterward, read and pray the following together:

In the name of the Father, and of the Son, and of the Holy Spirit:

My God, how great Thou art, how wonderful in all Thy works! Teach me Thy will that I may begin and end all my actions for Thy greater glory.

Amen.

St. John Neumann
Prayer found in *Bishop Neumann's Diary*

## Notes

# A TIME TO RETURN TO THE LIGHT

## 4th Sunday of Lent

*"The light came into the world, but people preferred darkness to light."*

*John 3:19*

*A Time to Return to the Light*

## Opening Prayer

Pray the following prayer together as a group. Notice the parts for the leader and for the rest of the group. This is the psalm we pray at Mass next Sunday. It describes feelings of Jerusalem temple musicians deported to Babylon after the Babylonians besieged their city and razed the temple.

In the name of the Father, and of the Son and of the Holy Spirit:

Psalm 137

**Leader:**

By the rivers of Babylon we sat mourning and weeping when we remembered Zion.
On the poplars of that land we hung up our harps.

**All:**

If I forget you, Jerusalem, may my right hand wither.

**Leader:**

There our captors asked us for the words of a song; our tormentors, for a joyful song: "Sing for us a song of Zion!"

**All:**

If I forget you, Jerusalem, may my right hand wither.

**Leader:**

But how could we sing a song of the LORD in a foreign land?

**All:**

If I forget you, Jerusalem, may my right hand wither.

**Leader:**

If I forget you, Jerusalem, may my right hand wither. May my tongue stick to my palate if I do not remember you, if I do not exalt Jerusalem beyond all my delights.

**All:**

If I forget you, Jerusalem, may my right hand wither.

## Introduction

1. Why would the musicians offer their right hands should they forget Jerusalem? Why the right hand?

2. Have you ever felt "exiled," or separated from loved ones or your home? The musicians coped by singing about their situation, and making promises to God. How do you cope with "exile?"

## A Time to Return to the Light

# Reading: John 3:14-21

**Have someone read the following passage aloud.**

"And as Moses lifted up the serpent in the wilderness, so must the Son of man be lifted up, [15]that whoever believes in him may have eternal life." [16]For God so loved the world that he gave his only Son, that whoever believes in him should not perish but have eternal life. [17]For God sent the Son into the world, not to condemn the world, but that the world might be saved through him. [18]He who believes in him is not condemned; he who does not believe is condemned already, because he has not believed in the name of the only Son of God. [19]And this is the judgment, that the light has come into the world, and men loved darkness rather than light, because their deeds were evil. [20]For every one who does evil hates the light, and does not come to the light, lest his deeds should be exposed. [21]But he who does what is true comes to the light, that it may be clearly seen that his deeds have been wrought in God."

> 3. What image does John the evangelist say Jesus gave for himself on the cross? How does this image strike you?

**Have someone read Numbers 21:4-9 aloud.**

*This Scripture occurs when the Israelites are wandering in the desert, after they have fled Pharaoh but not yet entered the promised land.*

[4]From Mount Hor they set out by the way to the Red Sea, to go around the land of Edom; and the people became impatient on the way. [5]And the people spoke against God and against Moses, "Why have you brought us up out of Egypt to die in the wilderness? For there is no food and no water, and we loathe this worthless food." [6]Then the LORD sent fiery serpents among the people, and they bit the people, so that many people of Israel died. [7]And the people came to Moses, and said, "We have sinned, for we have spoken against the LORD and against you; pray to the LORD, that he take away the serpents from

## 4th Sunday of Lent

us." So Moses prayed for the people. ⁸And the LORD said to Moses, "Make a fiery serpent, and set it on a pole; and every one who is bitten, when he sees it, shall live." ⁹So Moses made a bronze serpent, and set it on a pole; and if a serpent bit any man, he would look at the bronze serpent and live.

4. How would you describe the physical and mental state of the Israelites?

5. How do you think you would feel in their situation?

6. The word "exile" has powerful connotations from our salvation history. The temple musicians in Babylon are exiled from their home and the only place where they could worship. The Israelites in this excerpt from Numbers have fled Egypt but not yet reached the promised land. They have no home except the desert: the land of snakes and poisonous creatures.

   - If we look deeper into this story and take the snakes and bad food as metaphors, what experience of exile do you think they capture? For example, snakes can be scary – exile is scary.

   - Have you ever had a sense of being exiled from God? Or have you known anyone who has felt this?

   - What caused that feeling?

7. What evidence could you cite from your own observations of life that people prefer the darkness to the light? What ways do we seem to exile ourselves from God?

8. What is the evidence from Jesus' life that "the light came into the world, but people preferred darkness?"

9. If we prefer darkness to light, that means we choose it when we could choose the light. Have you ever known of someone who couldn't leave the darkness, who did not seem to have the power to move toward the light? What, if anything, did that person do to overcome? What might someone do?

### *A Time to Return to the Light*

10. If exile is a kind of darkness or isolation, then why don't we choose community, connection, relationship, interdependence? Why do we choose isolation?

11. How does John 3:20 explain the human tendency to choose darkness? Conversely, how does John 3:21 explain the motivation for trusting in Jesus?

12. If you've experienced a time when you have been motivated to move out of the darkness into the light of Jesus, what helped you to trust Jesus?

13. What made you recognize the darkness as darkness, the exile as exile?

## Reading: Ephesians: 2:4-10

**Have someone read the following passage aloud.**

[4]But God, who is rich in mercy, out of the great love with which he loved us, [5]even when we were dead through our trespasses, made us alive together with Christ (by grace you have been saved), [6]and raised us up with him, and made us sit with him in the heavenly places in Christ Jesus, [7]that in the coming ages he might show the immeasurable riches of his grace in kindness toward us in Christ Jesus. [8]For by grace you have been saved through faith; and this is not your own doing, it is the gift of God -- [9]not because of works, lest any man should boast. [10]For we are his workmanship, created in Christ Jesus for good works, which God prepared beforehand, that we should walk in them.

14. What are the specific ways outlined by St. Paul in which God is rich in mercy?

15. How could these aspects of mercy be used to give us or someone we love a pep talk about leaving the darkness and returning to the light that shines from our true home?

## Connection to the Cross This Week

- If you have not already received the Sacrament of Reconciliation this Lent, this would be a great time to do it. Reflect more deeply on how you feel exiled and why. Examine the dark corners of your life. Write down any insights and take them to the confessional. In doing so, you will expose these corners to the victorious light of Christ and begin experiencing healing in these areas.

- Re-read the Ephesians and Gospel readings from this study. Meditate on them more deeply. Allow God to fill you with hope through them.

- Spend time with the daily readings this week. If you would like more help praying them, Appendix A is a guide to *Lectio Divina,* the ancient practice of praying with the Scriptures. Taking up this practice can make your time with the Scriptures much more enriching.

- For a prayer specifically designed to help us in choosing light over dark, see Appendix C. It is a modified version of an extended mediation by St. Ignatius Loyola, the founder of the Jesuits. One of the reasons St. Ignatius of Loyola composed the *Spiritual Exercises* was to help people more deeply appreciate the state of the world, the particularities of their own nature, and what God's desire is of each person's life. "The Two Standards" is one of the exercises. A "standard" is a banner or flag on a field of battle. (Use of these is an ancient practice. Troops rallied around the banner after a battle.) Ignatius was a military man before his conversion. He used many battle images to guide prayer. In " The Two Standards" he asks us to imagine opposing forces of good and evil as armies on the battlefield, each gathered under its own flag, or standard. The army of darkness and the army of light stand opposed on the field of battle.

**This Week's Readings**

Monday - Isa 65:17-21; Ps 30:2+4, 5-6, 11-12a+13b; John 4:43-54
Tuesday - Ezek 47:1-9, 12; Ps 46:2-3, 5-6, 8-9; John 5:1-3a, 5-16
Wednesday - Isa 49:8-15; Ps 145:8-9, 13cd-14, 17-18; John 5:17-30
Thursday - Exod 32:7-14; Ps 106:19-20, 21-22, 23; John 5:31-47
Friday - Wis 2:1a, 12-22; Ps 34:17-18, 19-20, 21+23;
   John 7:1-2, 10, 25-30
Saturday - Jer 11:18-20; Ps 7:2-3, 9bc-10, 11-12; John 7:40-53

*4th Sunday of Lent*

## Closing Prayer

The facilitator could again first ask for any prayer petitions. The group could spend time praying for each other—perhaps everyone praying for the person on their right as in week one. Afterward pray the closing prayer aloud together.

In the name of the Father, and of the Son and of the Holy Spirit:

**Prayer of St. Francis**
Lord, make me an instrument of your Peace
Where there is hatred, let me sow love.
Where there is injury, pardon.
Where there is doubt, faith.
Where there is despair, hope.
Where there is darkness, light.
Where there is sadness, joy.
O Divine Master, grant that I may not so much seek
to be consoled as to console;
to be understood, as to understand;
to be loved, as to love;
for it is in giving that we receive,
it is in pardoning that we are pardoned
and it is in dying that we are born to Eternal Life.

Amen.

# Notes

# A TIME TO DIE

## 5th Sunday of Lent

*"'And I, when I am lifted up from the earth, will draw all men to myself.'"*

*John 12:32*

## Opening Prayer

**Have someone read the following prayer aloud.**

In the name of the Father, and of the Son, and of the Holy Spirit:

God our Father, we believe that you are here with us.

We gather as your sons and daughters, drawn by your Son and enlightened by the Holy Spirit.

Jesus, through our time together tonight, enable us to hear your invitation to follow you more courageously.

Holy Spirit, open our hearts to the Scriptures that through our meditation we might desire to give ourselves more fully and generously as Christ did to our Father.

We pray this through Christ, our Lord.

Amen.

# 5th Sunday of Lent

## Introduction

1. Can you think of a time when you did not give your full effort or fight hard enough for something important? How did that make you feel later? What would you have done differently?

## Scripture and Tradition

### Reading: Hebrews 5: 7-9

**Have someone read the following passage aloud.**

⁷In the days of his flesh, Jesus offered up prayers and supplications, with loud cries and tears, to him who was able to save him from death, and he was heard for his godly fear. ⁸Although he was a Son, he learned obedience through what he suffered; ⁹and being made perfect he became the source of eternal salvation to all who obey him…

### Reading: John 12: 20-33

**Have someone read the following passage aloud.**

²⁰Now among those who went up to worship at the feast were some Greeks. ²¹So these came to Philip, who was from Beth-saida in Galilee, and said to him, "Sir, we wish to see Jesus." ²²Philip went and told Andrew; Andrew went with Philip and they told Jesus. ²³And Jesus answered them, "The hour has come for the Son of man to be glorified. ²⁴Truly, truly, I say to you, unless a grain of wheat falls into the earth and dies, it remains alone; but if it dies, it bears much fruit. ²⁵He who

## A Time to Die

loves his life loses it, and he who hates his life in this world will keep it for eternal life. ²⁶If any one serves me, he must follow me; and where I am, there shall my servant be also; if any one serves me, the Father will honor him. ²⁷Now is my soul troubled. And what shall I say? 'Father, save me from this hour?' No, for this purpose I have come to this hour. ²⁸Father, glorify thy name." Then a voice came from heaven, "I have glorified it, and I will glorify it again." ²⁹The crowd standing by heard it and said that it had thundered. Others said, "An angel has spoken to him." ³⁰Jesus answered, "This voice has come for your sake, not for mine. ³¹Now is the judgment of this world, now shall the ruler of this world be cast out; ³²and I, when I am lifted up from the earth, will draw all men to myself." ³³He said this to show by what death he was to die.

2. What caught your attention in these readings?

3. What Lenten themes did you observe?

4. What sequence of events leads up to Jesus' speech? Why do you think the author provided so much detail? What might it mean that Greeks (non-Jews) were seeking Jesus?

5. How would you describe Jesus' tone and mood in the Gospel passage? Why do you think he speaks in this tone? How does this relate to the verses describing Jesus from the letter to the Hebrews?

6. What are some of the messages in Jesus' teachings in the Gospel (verses 24 - 26)? What do you think Jesus means when he says that if a seed dies, it bears much fruit or if you hate your life in this world you keep it for eternal life?

7. Do you think this frightened the disciples? Should it have frightened them?

8. How did Jesus live his own teachings? Looking to the Gospel and the letter to the Hebrews, how did Jesus battle the temptation to fear? Do you think he had to fight a fear of sacrificing himself completely?

## 5th Sunday of Lent

9. How have you experienced the necessity of putting to death the old for rebirth and renewal to occur?

10. What is the grain of wheat in your life right now? How are you being called to lose your life? What is the Lord calling you to put to death or lay down so that something new may come forth in you?

11. St. Catherine of Siena said that Jesus was never concerned about anything but the eternal Father's honor and the salvation of souls.[4] Yet we know that Jesus sympathizes with our weaknesses and was tempted in every way that we are, yet did not sin (cf. Heb 4:15).

    - How are both the temptations and the triumph of Christ present in these two readings?

    - What might we do practically to cling to Jesus more confidently through our daily weaknesses and our times of "loud cries and tears" (Heb 5:7), to let him be "the *source* of our eternal salvation" (Heb 5:9)?

12. What has helped you become more radical in your trust of God and your willingness to hand over the reins to God?

13. Where in your life might the Holy Spirit be calling you to press, explore, seek new depth, or lose yourself more fully? What glimpse, if any, do you have of the rebirth, the light, the newness of life that awaits you?

---

[4] From a letter to Frate Tommaso dalla Fonte, from *Letters of St. Catherine of Siena,* Vol. 2, translated by Suzanne Noffke, MRTS Volume 52 (Tempe, AZ, 1988), pp.695-696.

## Connection to the Cross This Week

- Take some time every day this week to ask yourself: to what do I cling instead of Christ? This might take many forms – food, human relationships, a false self, your own abilities, your spouse, or a habit of anxiety. Do this all week because the Lord may be the light of the world, but we have to give him enough time to allow him to penetrate the shadowy corners of our hearts and illuminate what hides there. Pray for him to ready you to understand the darkest shadows, where light penetrates only very slowly.

- Questions for you to examine in prayer this week: Jesus said that when he is lifted up, he will draw all men/women to himself.

    o What holds you back from being drawn more deeply into Christ?

    o What prevents you from opening or even flinging wide the doors to Christ?

    o What do you fear he would take away?

    o What do you find hard to believe?

    o Can you think of any lies of "the ruler of this world" that might impede you from cracking that door where Christ waits?

    o Who inspires you to believe that opening wide the door is not only worth it, but the greatest thing that could happen in your life?

## 5th Sunday of Lent

- Each day when you pray, after you have named something to which you cling, take that thing to Christ in prayer. You can do this with words, or visually. Say to him: Lord, this is something that keeps me from you, from peace, from living the life you mean me to live. Help me give this to you Lord. Please take it from me. I know it is not within my power to "fix" myself. Only your love can change this. I surrender it to you, oh Lord. Use words that come naturally to you. As it says in Appendix B, God wants the real you, not someone talking in a phony, affected or borrowed manner.

- To visualize giving this part of yourself to Christ, imagine him on the other side of a door. Stand on your side of the door, clinging to the thing that keeps you from opening it. Think of the ways you rely on this prop. Does it really accomplish what you want it to accomplish? Does it keep you safe, make you happy, prevent disaster, make you lovable? Try to identify all the hopes that you have placed in this behavior/state of mind/psychological propensity. When you can see that no matter what you believed it gave you in the past, it actually gives none of the things you really want, then you will be ready to open the door. Give this to the one standing on the other side, the one waiting to give you what you really need and who will help end the power this part of you has had in your life.

- If you make discoveries about yourself and your relationship with God through these prayer exercises, this week could be an ideal time to make your Lenten confession. If this doesn't seem the right thing to do, find some way to mark what you are trying to give over to God. This could be something more elaborate, such as writing God a letter about it, then burning it as an offering; or something as simple as taking a walk with God in one of your favorite places.

*A Time to Die*

**This Week's Readings**

Monday - Dan 13:1-9, 15-17, 19-30, 33-62 or 13:41c-62; Ps 23:1-3-6; John 8:1-11
Tuesday - Num 21:4-9; Ps 102:2-3, 16-18, 19-21; John 8:21-30
Wednesday - Dan 3:14-20, 91-92, 95; Dan 3:52, 53, 54, 55, 56; John 8:31-42
Thursday - Gen 17:3-9; Ps 105:4-5, 6-7, 8-9; John 8:51-59
Friday - Jer 20:10-13; Ps 18:2-3a, 3bc-4, 5-6, 7; John 10:31-42
Saturday - Ezek 37:21-28; Jer 31:10, 11-12abcd, 13; John 11:45-56

## Closing Prayer

**Read and pray the following aloud together:**

In the name of the Father, and of the Son, and of the Holy Spirit:

Lord, we want to give ourselves more fully to you.
You know that our faith is too small,
Our vision skewed,
And our fears great.
Grant us a supernatural outlook
So that we might see the grain of wheat in our lives
And want what you want.
Please make us more sensitive to your Holy Spirit
Who shows us how you draw us to yourself.
We do not want to miss your invitations.
Please help us to be faithful to your promptings.
We pray for the courage to be molded anew
And the trust to believe the promise of your glory.
We pray this through Christ our Lord.

Amen.

# Notes

# A TIME TO WEEP

## Palm Sunday of the Lord's Passion

*"I have offered my back to
those who struck me."* [5]

*Isaiah 50:6*

---
[5] Translation from the *New Jerusalem Bible*.

## Opening Prayer

Read the following prayer together as a group.

**Palm Sunday Liturgy Opening Prayer**

In the name of the Father, and of the Son, and of the Holy Spirit:

Almighty, ever-living God, you have given the human race Jesus Christ our Savior as a model of humility. He fulfilled your will by becoming man and giving his life on the cross. Help us to bear witness to you by following his example of suffering, and make us worthy to share in his resurrection. We ask this through our Lord Jesus Christ, your Son, who lives and reigns with you and the Holy Spirit, one God, for ever and ever.

Amen.

*Palm Sunday of the Lord's Passion*

## Introduction

1. Have you had a powerful experience relating the Passion to your life?

2. What scene of the Passion narrative has spoken most powerfully to you in the past?

## Scripture and Tradition

**Have someone read the following aloud.**

The readings are long, but worth the time. Nothing but Scripture itself describes so starkly what happened to Jesus that Good Friday nearly 2000 years ago, especially Mark's gospel. Read slowly. Allow time for silence where indicated, and wherever else you think appropriate. The citation for the full gospel reading is at the beginning, but only the sections on which questions are provided appear below. This will allow for prayer and consideration over key moments.

## Reading: Mark 14:1 – 15:47

**Have someone read the following passage aloud.**

[17]And when it was evening he came with the twelve. [18]And as they were at table eating, Jesus said, "Truly, I say to you, one of you will betray me, one who is eating with me." [19]They began to be sorrowful, and to say to him one after another, "Is it I?" [20]He said to them, "It is one of the twelve, one who is dipping bread into the dish with me. [21]For the Son of man goes as it is written of him, but woe to that man by whom

the Son of man is betrayed! It would have been better for that man if he had not been born." ²²And as they were eating, he took bread, and blessed, and broke it, and gave it to them, and said, "Take; this is my body." ²³And he took a cup, and when he had given thanks he gave it to them, and they all drank of it. ²⁴And he said to them, "This is my blood of the covenant, which is poured out for many. ²⁵Truly, I say to you, I shall not drink again of the fruit of the vine until that day when I drink it new in the kingdom of God." ²⁶And when they had sung a hymn, they went out to the Mount of Olives. ²⁷And Jesus said to them, "You will all fall away; for it is written, ' I will strike the shepherd, and the sheep will be scattered.' ²⁸But after I am raised up, I will go before you to Galilee." ²⁹Peter said to him, "Even though they all fall away, I will not." ³⁰And Jesus said to him, "Truly, I say to you, this very night, before the cock crows twice, you will deny me three times." ³¹But he said vehemently, "If I must die with you, I will not deny you." And they all said the same.

3. Why do you think Jesus told his disciples that one of them would betray him? Since it seems to be inevitable, what would have made Jesus inform his followers of this?

4. Here is the first celebration of the Lord's Supper and the institution of the Sacrament of Eucharist. What do you think the disciples thought when Jesus was blessing and sharing the meal with these words?

5. How would you describe Peter's declaration: "I will not deny you?" What motivates such a comment? What would have been Peter's state of mind when he said it?

**Have someone read the following passage aloud.**

³²And they went to a place which was called Gethsemane; and he said to his disciples, "Sit here, while I pray." ³³And he took with him Peter and James and John, and began to be greatly distressed and troubled. ³⁴And he said to them, "My soul is very sorrowful, even to death; remain here, and watch." ³⁵And going a little farther, he fell on the ground and prayed that, if it were possible, the hour might pass from him. ³⁶And he

said, "Abba, Father, all things are possible to thee; remove this cup from me; yet not what I will, but what thou wilt." [37]And he came and found them sleeping, and he said to Peter, "Simon, are you asleep? Could you not watch one hour? [38]Watch and pray that you may not enter into temptation; the spirit indeed is willing, but the flesh is weak." [39]And again he went away and prayed, saying the same words. [40]And again he came and found them sleeping, for their eyes were very heavy; and they did not know what to answer him. [41]And he came the third time, and said to them, "Are you still sleeping and taking your rest? It is enough; the hour has come; the Son of man is betrayed into the hands of sinners. [42]Rise, let us be going; see, my betrayer is at hand."

6. How do you think the three apostles who saw the transfiguration and now accompany Jesus to Gethsemane felt when Jesus said: "My soul is sorrowful, even unto death"?

7. Do you think they meant to stay awake?

8. Jesus falls on the ground when he goes to pray. What does that indicate about his state of mind and the prayer he prays?

9. How do you think the disciples would have felt looking back on their last hour with Jesus at Gethsemane?

10. Have you ever offered a prayer in the midst of distress? What did your prayer sound like? Would you care to share that experience? What do you think Jesus' tone would have been in praying to God to let this cup pass him by?

**Have someone read the following introduction and passage aloud.**

[43]And immediately, while he was still speaking, Judas came, one of the twelve, and with him a crowd with swords and clubs, from the chief priests and the scribes and the elders. [44]Now the betrayer had given them a sign, saying, "The one I shall kiss is the man; seize him and lead him away under guard." [45]And when he came, he went up to him at

### A Time to Weep

once, and said, "Master!" And he kissed him. ⁴⁶And they laid hands on him and seized him. ⁴⁷But one of those who stood by drew his sword, and struck the slave of the high priest and cut off his ear. ⁴⁸And Jesus said to them, "Have you come out as against a robber, with swords and clubs to capture me? ⁴⁹Day after day I was with you in the temple teaching, and you did not seize me. But let the scriptures be fulfilled." ⁵⁰And they all forsook him, and fled. ⁵¹And a young man followed him, with nothing but a linen cloth about his body; and they seized him, ⁵²but he left the linen cloth and ran away naked.

11. Mark is the only evangelist who tells of the young man wearing only a linen cloth who runs off naked when the mob tries to grab him. What do you think this adds to the story?

12. Christian tradition has held that this young man was Mark himself, the gospel writer. Does that change your sense of why he included this story? What does it say about his role in the scene? How do you think he felt about what he did if it was him?

⁶⁰And the high priest stood up in the midst, and asked Jesus, "Have you no answer to make? What is it that these men testify against you?" ⁶¹But he was silent and made no answer. Again the high priest asked him, "Are you the Christ, the Son of the Blessed?" ⁶²And Jesus said, "I am; and you will see the Son of man seated at the right hand of Power, and coming with the clouds of heaven." ⁶³And the high priest tore his garments, and said, "Why do we still need witnesses? ⁶⁴You have heard his blasphemy. What is your decision?" And they all condemned him as deserving death. ⁶⁵And some began to spit on him, and to cover his face, and to strike him, saying to him, "Prophesy!" And the guards received him with blows.

13. What do you think about Jesus' answer to Caiaphas' question? What does it tell you about Jesus? His intentions, principles, identity?

14. What emotions might have been behind his determination that Jesus should die? How would you explain the viciousness of the attacks on Jesus after he speaks?

## Palm Sunday of the Lord's Passion

**Have someone read the following passage aloud.**

[16]And the soldiers led him away inside the palace (that is, the praetorium); and they called together the whole battalion. [17]And they clothed him in a purple cloak, and plaiting a crown of thorns they put it on him. [18]And they began to salute him, "Hail, King of the Jews!" [19]And they struck his head with a reed, and spat upon him, and they knelt down in homage to him. [20]And when they had mocked him, they stripped him of the purple cloak, and put his own clothes on him. And they led him out to crucify him. [21]And they compelled a passer-by, Simon of Cyrene, who was coming in from the country, the father of Alexander and Rufus, to carry his cross.

**Have someone else read aloud the following passage.**

> Here the greatest mystery of all time was revealed to us: God chose to reveal the divine glory to us in humiliation. Where all beauty if gone, all eloquence silenced, all splendor taken away, and all admiration withdrawn, there it is that God has chosen to manifest unconditional love to us.
>
> Henri M. Nouwen and Helen David
> *Walk With Jesus: Stations of the Cross*

**Leader, please take the group slowly through the following prayer exercise:**

Please close your eyes and sit quietly for a moment to empty your mind.

Imagine you are Simon the Cyrene, a man with business in Jerusalem. You're on your way about your errands, possibly accompanied by your sons, Alexander and Rufus (Mark 15:21). A noisy crowd approaches – another crucifixion. Suddenly someone grabs you, throws a cross on your shoulder because the man being crucified today can carry it no further. He is black and blue from beating and bleeding from whips and thorns.

## A Time to Weep

15. **What thoughts flash instantly through your head? (Allow a minute of silence.)**

16. **Look Jesus, beaten and broken, in the eyes. (Allow another minute of silence.)**

17. **Please open your eyes. Let's discuss our thoughts after looking at Jesus. How were they different from your first? Did anyone have any special insight they want to share?**

**Have someone read the following passage aloud.**

**When you reach the moment at verse 37 when Jesus dies, please allow a minute of silence.**

²²And they brought him to the place called Golgotha (which means the place of a skull). ²³And they offered him wine mingled with myrrh; but he did not take it. ²⁴And they crucified him, and divided his garments among them, casting lots for them, to decide what each should take. ²⁵And it was the third hour, when they crucified him. ²⁶And the inscription of the charge against him read, "The King of the Jews." ²⁷And with him they crucified two robbers, one on his right and one on his left. ²⁹And those who passed by derided him, wagging their heads, and saying, "Aha! You who would destroy the temple and build it in three days, ³⁰save yourself, and come down from the cross!" ³¹So also the chief priests mocked him to one another with the scribes, saying, "He saved others; he cannot save himself. ³²Let the Christ, the King of Israel, come down now from the cross, that we may see and believe." Those who were crucified with him also reviled him. ³³And when the sixth hour had come, there was darkness over the whole land until the ninth hour. ³⁴And at the ninth hour Jesus cried with a loud voice, "Elo-i, Elo-i, lama sabach-thani?" which means, "My God, my God, why hast thou forsaken me?" ³⁵And some of the bystanders hearing it said, "Behold, he is calling Elijah." ³⁶And one ran and, filling a sponge full of vinegar, put it on a reed and gave it to him to drink, saying, "Wait, let us see whether Elijah will come to take him down." ³⁷And Jesus uttered a loud cry, and breathed his last.

## SILENCE

³⁸And the curtain of the temple was torn in two, from top to bottom. ³⁹And when the centurion, who stood facing him, saw that he thus breathed his last, he said, "Truly this man was the Son of God!" ⁴⁰There were also women looking on from afar, among whom were Mary Magdalene, and Mary the mother of James the younger and of Joses, and Salome, ⁴¹who, when he was in Galilee, followed him, and ministered to him; and also many other women who came up with him to Jerusalem. ⁴²And when evening had come, since it was the day of Preparation, that is, the day before the sabbath, ⁴³Joseph of Arimathea, a respected member of the council, who was also himself looking for the kingdom of God, took courage and went to Pilate, and asked for the body of Jesus. ⁴⁴And Pilate wondered if he were already dead; and summoning the centurion, he asked him whether he was already dead. ⁴⁵And when he learned from the centurion that he was dead, he granted the body to Joseph. ⁴⁶And he bought a linen shroud, and taking him down, wrapped him in the linen shroud, and laid him in a tomb which had been hewn out of the rock; and he rolled a stone against the door of the tomb. ⁴⁷Mary Magdalene and Mary the mother of Joses saw where he was laid.

19. Do you think the chief priests and elders felt they had triumphed when Jesus was dead? Do you think their feelings were more complex? What would have influenced their feelings?

20. Were you able to focus on the death of Jesus in the silence?

21. Only Mark's gospels says that Joseph of Arimathea "took courage" (vs. 44). Why would it require courage? What does that imply about the situation of the friends of Jesus vis-à-vis Pilate?

22. Did you experience anything you hadn't previously in regard to Jesus' death? If so and you're comfortable sharing, please tell us about it.

*A Time to Weep*

## Connection to the Cross This Week

- The celebrations of the sacred Triduum are our high holy days. Observing them has the power to bring us into the mystery of Christ's death and resurrection as nothing else can.

This week, commit to attending the Mass of the Lord's supper on Thursday night, when the Church marks the last supper by washing feet. The rite calls for the consecrated bread to be removed from the Church and taken to a chapel of repose, where we can watch and pray with Jesus in the garden of Gethsemane. The tabernacle is left open to reveal a void, as Jesus emptied himself for us. Meditate on the hymn from Philippians 2 that we read at Passion Sunday Mass: Christ

> …did not count equality with God a thing to be grasped: but emptied himself, taking the form of a servant, being born in the likeness of men. And being found in human form he humbled himself and became obedient unto death, even death on a cross.

Consider the emptiness Christ knew standing before the courts, in the praetorium, carrying his cross, nailed to it on Golgotha. Empty yourself to share in his emptiness.

Participate in this vigil with your whole heart. Watch and pray with him.

At the Good Friday prayer service, we commemorate the day of Jesus' suffering. The passion according to John is read, or often sung. The consecrated bread from Holy Thursday's Mass is distributed. We venerate the cross, the reminder of what Christ underwent for our salvation.

## *Palm Sunday of the Lord's Passion*

On Holy Saturday, new Christians are brought into the Church at the Great Vigil. This service includes seven readings from the Old Testament, two from the new, baptisms, confirmations, and first Eucharist for the neophytes. It is a long service, but it never seems too long. Adult baptism can be one of the most powerful rites one will ever witness. If you can attend this service, do!

- Monday through Friday, meditate for at least ten minutes each day on the following passage. Consider your own death, as well as Jesus dying on the cross.

    We all must die. And we all will die alone. No one can make that final journey with us. We have to let go of what is most our own and trust that we did not live in vain. Somehow, dying is the greatest of all human moments because it is the moment in which we are asked to give everything. The way we die has not only much to do with the way we have lived, but also with the way those who come after us will live. Jesus' death reveals to us that we do not have to live pretending that death is not something that comes to all of us. As his hands stretched out between heaven and earth, he asks us to look our mortality straight in the face and trust that death does not have the last word. We can then look at the dying in our world and give them hope; we can hold their dying bodies in our arms and trust that mightier arms than ours will receive them and give them the peace and joy they always desire.

    In dying, all of humanity is one. And it was into this dying humanity that God entered so as to give us hope.

    Nouwen and David, pp 70 – 71<br>*Walk With Jesus*

## A Time to Weep

**This Week's Readings**

Monday – Isa 42:1-7; Ps 27:1, 2, 3, 13-14; John 12:1-11
Tuesday – Isa 49:1-6; Ps 71:1-2, 3-4a, 5-6ab, 15+17;
　John 13:21-33, 36-38
Wednesday – Isa 50:4-9a; Ps 69:8-10, 21-22, 31+33-34;
　Matt 26:14-25
Holy Thursday – Ex 12:1-8, 11-14; Ps 116:12-13, 15-16bc, 17-18;
　1 Cor 11:23-26; Jn 13:1-15
Good Friday – Isa 52:13-53:12; Ps 3:2, 6, 12-13, 15-16, 17, 25
Holy Saturday – Gen 1:1-22; Gen 22:1-18; Isa 54:5-14; Isa 55:1-11;
　Bar 3:9-15, 32; Ez 36:16- 28; Isa 12:2-6; Roman 6:3-11; Mk 16:1-7

## Closing Prayer

**Pray the following together. You could alternate paragraphs between individuals.**

In the name of the Father, and of the Son, and of the Holy Spirit:

### I Thirst
by Blessed Theresa of Calcutta (**Mother Teresa**)

[Jesus says to us...]
　It is true. I stand at the door of your heart, day and night. Even when you are not listening, even when you doubt it could be Me, I am there. I await even the smallest sign of your response, even the least whispered invitation that will allow Me to enter.

## Palm Sunday of the Lord's Passion

I know what is in your heart – I know your loneliness and all your hurts – the rejections, the judgments, the humiliations, I carried it all before you. And I carried it all for you, so you might share My strength and victory. I know especially your need for love – how you are thirsting to be loved and cherished. But how often have you thirsted in vain, by seeking that love selfishly,
striving to fill the emptiness inside you with passing pleasures – with the even greater emptiness of sin. Do you thirst for love? "Come to Me all you who thirst…" (Jn. 7: 37). I will satisfy you and fill you. Do you thirst to be cherished? I cherish you more than you can imagine – to the point of dying on a cross for you.

Don't you realize that My Father already has a perfect plan to transform your life, beginning from this moment? Trust in Me. Ask Me every day to enter and take charge of your life – and I will. I promise you before My Father in heaven that I will work miracles in your life. Why would I do this? Because I THIRST FOR YOU. All I ask of you is that you entrust yourself to Me completely. I will do all the rest.

**Pray aloud together:**
Jesus, thank you for your great love, poured out for us on the cross. Please give us the grace to entrust ourselves completely to you as we prepare for your resurrection. We ask this all in the name of the Father, and of the Son, and of the Holy Spirit. Amen.

# Notes

# A TIME TO TRULY LIVE

## Easter Sunday: The Resurrection of the Lord

*"You have been raised with Christ."*

*Colossians 3:1*

*A Time to Truly Live*

## Opening Prayer

This could be read responsorially, with half the group praying a couplet, the other half praying the next. All should pray together after "let us pray," or one could pray this for the group.

### The *"Anima Christi"* of St. Elizabeth Ann Seton

In the name of the Father, and of the Son, and of the Holy Spirit.

Soul of Jesus,
Sanctify me.

Blood of Jesus,
Wash me,

Passion of Jesus,
Comfort me.

Wounds of Jesus,
Hide me.

Heart of Jesus,
Receive me.

Spirit of Jesus,
Enliven me.

## Easter Sunday

Goodness of Jesus,
Pardon me.

Beauty of Jesus,
Draw me.

Humility of Jesus,
Humble me.

Peace of Jesus,
Pacify me.

Love of Jesus,
Inflame me.

Kingdom of Jesus,
Come to me.

Grace of Jesus,
Replenish me.

Mercy of Jesus,
Pity me.

Sanctity of Jesus,
Sanctify me.

Purity of Jesus,
Purify me.

Cross of Jesus,
Support me.

Nails of Jesus,
Hold me.

Mouth of Jesus,
Bless me in life, in death, in time and eternity.

Mouth of Jesus,
Defend me in the hour of death.

Mouth of Jesus,
Call me to come to Thee.

Mouth of Jesus,
Receive me with Thy saints in glory evermore.

Let Us Pray

Unite me to Thyself,
O adorable Victim.
Life-giving heavenly Bread,
feed me,
sanctify me,
reign in me,
transform me to Thyself,
live in me;

## Easter Sunday

let me live in Thee;
let me adore Thee in Thy life-giving Sacrament as my God,
listen to Thee as to my Master,
obey Thee as my King,
imitate Thee as my Model,
follow Thee as my Shepherd,
love Thee as my Father,
seek Thee as my Physician
who wilt heal all the maladies of my soul.
Be indeed my Way,
Truth and Life;
sustain me,
O heavenly Manna,
through the desert of this world,
till I shall behold Thee unveiled in Thy glory.

Amen.

## Introduction

1. Has anyone ever experienced a radical change in their lives? How did that change come about?

2. Did that change make others uncomfortable?

*A Time to Truly Live*

## Scripture and Tradition

**Read aloud.**

In the context of our reading from Acts, Peter has a vision that teaches him all food is clean. (Jewish dietary laws stipulated some food was "unclean" and should never be eaten.)

After this vision, the servants of Cornelius summon Peter. Cornelius is described as "a Centurion, an upright and God-fearing man." (Acts 10:22) A "holy angel" had instructed Cornelius to summon Peter and listen to him. While Peter is fetched, Cornelius' friends are invited to his house too. That means Peter is probably speaking to a group of soldiers, their wives and children, and possibly Roman government administrators who might have been in Jerusalem as part of the imperial occupation.

This vision of Peter, the leader designated by Christ, becomes a catalyst for the earliest followers of Jesus. Through it they learn that God desires dietary and other laws of the old covenant should not be impediments to the "nations" entering into this new baptized life offered in Christ. (Nations is generally translated "gentiles." It means all non-Jewish people.)

## Reading: Acts 10:34a, 37-43

**Have someone read the following passage aloud.**

³⁴And Peter opened his mouth and said: . . . ³⁷"the word which was proclaimed throughout all Judea, beginning from Galilee after the baptism which John preached: ³⁸how God anointed Jesus of Nazareth with the Holy Spirit and with power; how he went about doing good and heal-

## Easter Sunday

ing all that were oppressed by the devil, for God was with him. ³⁹And we are witnesses to all that he did both in the country of the Jews and in Jerusalem. They put him to death by hanging him on a tree; ⁴⁰but God raised him on the third day and made him manifest; ⁴¹not to all the people but to us who were chosen by God as witnesses, who ate and drank with him after he rose from the dead. ⁴²And he commanded us to preach to the people, and to testify that he is the one ordained by God to be judge of the living and the dead. ⁴³To him all the prophets bear witness that every one who believes in him receives forgiveness of sins through his name."

3. As a Jew, Peter was forbidden to fraternize with gentiles. What impression do you think Peter's visit to Cornelius and company would have made on observant Jews? Those who heard Peter? The other apostles and disciples?

4. What do you think Peter's thoughts might have been as he accompanied the servants to Cornelius' home?

5. What do you think he would have needed to believe, despite any misgivings, in order to do something that his whole life he had thought was wrong?

6. Does your understanding of what is right and good ever conflict with social norms and mores? Please explain.

7. Why do you think the Church has us read this story on Easter day?

8. The word "witness" appears three times in this reading. Look at what the word means in each instance. Is each meaning the same as the others?

9. How do you witness in your own life?

*A Time to Truly Live*

# Reading: John 20:1-9

**Have someone read the following passage aloud.**

[1]Now on the first day of the week Mary Magdalene came to the tomb early, while it was still dark, and saw that the stone had been taken away from the tomb. [2]So she ran, and went to Simon Peter and the other disciple, the one whom Jesus loved, and said to them, "They have taken the Lord out of the tomb, and we do not know where they have laid him." [3]Peter then came out with the other disciple, and they went toward the tomb. [4]They both ran, but the other disciple outran Peter and reached the tomb first; [5]and stooping to look in, he saw the linen cloths lying there, but he did not go in. [6]Then Simon Peter came, following him, and went into the tomb; he saw the linen cloths lying, [7]and the napkin, which had been on his head, not lying with the linen cloths but rolled up in a place by itself. [8]Then the other disciple, who reached the tomb first, also went in, and he saw and believed; [9]for as yet they did not know the scripture, that he must rise from the dead.

10. Why do you think Mary Magdalene went to the tomb that morning? What reasons does someone today go to a grave site soon after a death?

11. Why do you think "the disciple Jesus loved" would not go into the tomb even though he arrived first?

12. Imagine that you didn't know the Easter story. What are some thoughts the apostle whom Jesus loved might have had when, standing alone at the entrance to the tomb, he saw the burial cloths?

13. Why do you think John notes that both Peter and the beloved disciple saw the burial clothes?

## Easter Sunday

**Read aloud.**

Carlo Carretto was headed into a political career until the fascists took over the Italian government. Instead he threw himself into Catholic Action, a youth movement that sought to mobilize laity to advance the religious and social priorities of the Church.

After spending twenty years in a blur of meetings, conferences and public organizing, he left it all to become a contemplative in the desert of North Africa. He became a Little Brothers of Jesus, followers of St. Charles de Foucauld.

Eventually Carretto returned to Italy to found a community where lay people could participate with the brothers in prayer and reflection. He was a popular retreat master and the author of many books, most famously *Letters from the Desert* which describes his years in an Algerian monastery.

**Have someone read aloud the following selection from Carretto's writing.**

> Real death is separation from God, and this is unbearable; real death is faithlessness, hopelessness and lovelessness....
>
> Real death is the chaos where human beings find themselves when they disobey the Father, it is the tangled web to which they are reduced by their passions, it is the total defeat of all their dreams of greatness, it is the disintegration of their whole personality.
>
> Real death is emptiness, darkness, desolation, despair, hatred, destruction. So...Christ agreed to enter this death, into this separation, so as to identify himself with all who were in separation, and to save them.

## A Time to Truly Live

When he touched the depths of their despair he announced hope with his resurrection.

When he was immersed in their darkness he made the brightness of the truth burst forth with his resurrection.

When engulfed by the abyss of their lovelessness he showed them the infinite joy of love with his resurrection.

By rising from the dead he made all things new.

By rising from the dead he opened new heavens.

By rising from the dead he opened new life.

*Carlo Carretto: Selected Writings*

## Reading: Colossians 3:1-4

**Have someone read the following passage aloud.**

[1]If then you have been raised with Christ, seek the things that are above, where Christ is, seated at the right hand of God. [2]Set your minds on things that are above, not on things that are on earth. [3]For you have died, and your life is hid with Christ in God. [4]When Christ who is our life appears, then you also will appear with him in glory.

14. Keeping in mind Carlo Carretto's words about what death is, what does it mean to you to be raised with Christ from the dead? (Col 3:1)

15. Has reflecting on Jesus' words and deeds this Lent changed or added in anyway to what it means to be raised with Christ?

16. Do you believe yourself raised?

---

[5]Orbis: Maryknoll, NY, 1994, p. 147, 8.

*Easter Sunday*

17. **St. Paul wrote to the Corinthians:** "If any one is in Christ, he is a new creation; the old has passed away, behold, the new has come." (2 Cor 5:17) How can we more fully embrace the power of the resurrection to overcome old habits of being and truly live as a new creation?

## Connection to the Cross This Year

Have someone read the following aloud.

Sometimes we don't feel much like resurrection people, born anew. The parts of our lives that most need regeneration also seem the most entrenched. Some are deeply embedded in our spirits because they were formed in childhood as ways to deal with difficult situations, yet they don't serve us well as adults. Some seem so much a part of our personalities that we feel we would not be ourselves without them, no matter how much they hurt us.

Embrace the power of the resurrection in a new way this year. Pick one part of your life where you feel a pressing need to become a new creation, to let the old die off and something new be born. Commit that part of your life to prayer. Use a search engine such as Biblegateway.com to find Scriptures that pertain to this part of your life. Pray over each one for a week.

Seek to acquire "a fresh, spiritual way of thinking" in regard to this recalcitrant area of your life. (Ephesians 4:23) We can feel confident this is possible because St. Paul assures us that "the weapons of our warfare have divine power to destroy strongholds." (2 Cor 10:4) God has power over every part of our lives if we invite him into the places that don't work right and surrender to his loving action.

But we have to cooperate. St. Paul says we "take every thought captive to obey Christ." (2 Cor 10: 5b) The old, unresurrected men and women will not die if we continue to harbor their thoughts. Developing "a fresh way of thinking" requires fresh thoughts!

Watching our thoughts requires careful attention only possible if one has a solid prayer life. Commit yourself to twenty minutes of time with the Lord everyday. This time will allow God to carve out the space within you where he can dwell. It's that God-created space that will help you observe and gain power over your thoughts.[6]

The goal isn't self-help or self-improvement. We'll be improved, not because of what we do, but because of what God did in Christ and so does in us, making us new creations. We are a resurrection people! Live it!

---

[6]Two books by a Benedictine nun are helpful: *Thoughts Matter* and *Tools Matter for Practicing the Spiritual Life* by Mary Margaret Funk. She distills and makes comprehensible for the modern person the thought of the ancient monastic tradition. See also *Battlefield of the Mind* by Joyce Meyer.

## Closing Prayer

The facilitator could again ask for any prayer petitions that people have. The group could spend time praying for each other—perhaps again having everyone pray for the person on their right. Then pray the Closing Prayer aloud together.

**Thomas Merton's Prayer**

MY LORD GOD, I have no idea where I am going.
I do not see the road ahead of me.
I cannot know for certain where it will end.
Nor do I really know myself, and the fact that I think that I am following your will does not mean that I am actually doing so.
But I believe that the desire to please you does in fact please you.
And I hope I have that desire in all that I am doing.
I hope that I will never do anything apart from that desire.
And I know that if I do this you will lead me by the right road though I may know nothing about it.
Therefore will I trust you always though I may seem to be lost and in the shadow of death.
I will not fear, for you are ever with me, and you will never leave me to face my perils alone.

Thomas Merton
*Thoughts in Solitude*

APPENDIX A

# A Guide to *Lectio Divina* (Divine Reading)

*Lectio Divina* is the ancient method of praying Scripture that monastics and others have practiced for centuries

*Lectio Divina* is composed of four steps:
1. Reading *(lectio)*
2. Meditation *(meditatio)*
3. Prayer *(oratio)*
4. Contemplation *(contemplatio)*

## Reading *(lectio)*

Choose a text of the Scriptures. In this study, we provide you with the daily readings at the end of each "Connection to the Cross This Week" section. Often, though, Scripture that is particularly relevant to our life concerns will help us to commit to the practice. God uses what is relevant to speak to us directly.

Place yourself in a comfortable position and allow yourself to become silent. Read the text, slowly. Savor each portion of the reading, constantly listening for the "still small voice" of a word or phrase that somehow says "I am for you today." Do not expect lightening or ecstasies. In *lectio divina* God is teaching us to listen to him, to seek him in the word. He does not reach out and grab us; rather, he softly, gently invites us ever more deeply into his presence.

Read the passage again out loud, then allow more time for the word to penetrate your heart and mind. After you have allowed time to absorb it, read it one more time, either silently or out loud. Look for a word or phrase that God might be speaking to you.

## Meditation *(meditatio)*

Take the word or phrase into yourself. Memorize it and slowly repeat it to yourself, allowing it to interact with your inner world of concerns, memories and ideas. Do not be afraid of "distractions." Memories or thoughts are simply parts of yourself which, when they rise up during prayer, are asking to be given to God along with the rest of your inner self. Allow this inner pondering, this rumination, to invite you into dialogue with God.

### Prayer *(oratio)*

Now speak to God. Whether you use words or ideas or images or all three is not important. Interact with God as you would with one who you know loves and accepts you. Give him what you have discovered in yourself during your experience of meditation. Experience God using the word or phrase that he has given you as a means of blessing, of transforming the ideas and memories which your pondering on his word has awakened. Give to God what you have found within your heart.

### Contemplation *(contemplatio)*

Finally, simply rest in God's embrace. And when he invites you to return to your pondering of his word or to your inner dialogues with him, do so. Learn to use words when words are helpful, and to let go of words when they no longer are necessary. Rejoice in the knowledge that God is with you in both words and silence, in spiritual activity and inner receptivity.

Sometimes in *lectio divina* one will return several times to the printed text, either to savor the literary context of the word or phrase that God has given, or to seek a new word or phrase to ponder. At other times only a single word or phrase will fill the whole time set aside for *lectio divina*. It is not necessary to anxiously assess the quality of one's *lectio divina* as if one were "performing" or seeking some goal: *lectio divina* has no goal other than that of being in the presence of God by praying the Scriptures.

This was adapted from an article by Fr. Luke Dysinger, O.S.B. For the full article, see St. Andrew's Abbey Homepage, www.valyermo.com/index.html

# APPENDIX B

# Learning to Listen to God

## App B: Learning to Listen to God

Mass is designed to help us receive from God. Daily Mass is a sure way to spend most of a half-hour in quiet prayer. If you can't get to daily Mass, don't worry. God wants to meet you wherever you seek him.

Find any place where you can sit quietly, undisturbed for 20 minutes. Ideally we create a prayer space in our homes. Just entering that chair, or lighting the candle, helps signal our bodies it is time to be with God. Not everyone has a home where that luxury is possible. If not, the outdoors is often one of the best places for silence with God. The grandeur of nature silences our minds, and we are usually certain not to be interrupted. A tree can become a fine prayer partner!

Start by trying to relax your body and mind as much as possible. Some people will go through tightening the muscles for 10 seconds of tension in each part of their body, then releasing for ten seconds, starting from the bottom and working up: feet, calves, thighs, tummy, chest, arms, neck, and head. This is both a relaxing and a focusing exercise.

Always begin prayer by recognizing in some way that God is real and really with you. "Lord, you are all powerful, greater than I can ever conceive. I want to be with you." Use words that are natural and comfortable for you. God wants the real you, not you speaking in some unfamiliar strained voice.

> *Pray in all simplicity… The publican and the thief were reconciled by a single utterance. In your prayers there is no need for high-flown words, for it is the simple babblings of children that have more often won the heart of the Father in Heaven.*
>
> St. John Climacus, *The Ladder of Divine Ascent*

Sometimes people feel awkward about telling God who he is, yet Christians have done so for thousands of years. (See the psalms for examples.) These words honor God, but also remind us of who God is and what we believe about God. Does God need our praise? Of course not. God is beyond need. We need to praise!

Praying a prayer of the Church is a sure fire way to focus our quiet time on God: the Our Father, the Divine Praises, the *Anima Christi*. All of these are available online if you don't know them.

Next, offer the prayer time to God. He is the one that will make something of it, not us. You might even say: "I give this time to you, oh God. Do with it what you will." This takes the pressure off you to "perform" by controlling your thoughts, or to have particular feelings.

One of the most important things to know in entering more seriously into prayer is that most prayers are not about feelings. Yes, we often go to the Lord when we have strong feelings, but what kind of relationship would you have with a person you went to only for help? That person might be your professional counselor or advisor, but you don't have a real friendship with them. Jesus called us friends, not clients.

Sometimes in silent prayer you might well feel bored, empty or dry. All of the great writers on prayer discuss this. It doesn't mean that God isn't doing something with the time you give. Think of time you have with your closest friends and family. Does not real intimacy involve just being together, sometimes in boredom and discomfort, sometimes in intense conversation, sometimes just in love?

God might occasionally give us what is traditionally known as "consolation," but that is not the purpose of prayer. The purpose is a relationship with God in Christ. We know that any relationship to which we give significant time and attention has effects on us: so too, a relationship with God. The effects of a relationship with God are far, far beyond those we have with other people. God is the only one able to give "the peace beyond all understanding" (Philippians 4:6-7).

If we give God the time that makes a relationship possible, God will carve out the space within you where the Holy Spirit will dwell, and change your life.

Christian silent prayer is different than eastern meditation. The point

## App B: Learning to Listen to God

is not to empty yourself for the sake of emptying. As Thomas Keating, O.C.S.O. writes in his great work, *Open Mind, Open Heart*:

> Please don't try to make your faculties a blank. There should always be a gentle, spiritual activity present, expressed either by thinking the sacred word[7] or by the simple awareness that you are present to God… This prayer is a way of resting in God.
>
> Thomas Keating, *Open Mind, Open Heart*, p. 38

If distractions come, good for you for noticing! Simply refocus yourself. St. Teresa of Avila, the great teacher of prayer, wrote that she had made a wonderful discovery: prayer happens even though the faculties are busy elsewhere. "The clacking old mill (thought) must keep on going round" (*Interior Castle* 4, 79). "Let her laugh at it as at an idiot and keep her peace" (*Way of Perfection* 33, 24).

St. Teresa's words, though not as sensitive as a modern person's might be, are as relevant today as when she wrote them. Think for a moment how kind you would be to someone with a cognitive disability who talks incessantly. That is what our minds do! Try to be as kind to yourself about your mind wandering as you would be to someone you knew couldn't help his behavior.

A great modern writer on prayer, Carmelite nun Ruth Burrows, O.C.D. (*Guidelines to Mystical Prayer*) compares the mind's incessant jumping from thought to thought to our faculty for hearing. An ear cannot stop hearing. If noise happens nearby, our ears will perceive it; so too, the mind. Unless God stills our faculties (stops our thoughts), they will run hither and yon. Trust that God will arrest your faculties if you're ever ready for that perfect stillness, and thank God that he doesn't give you what you're not ready to receive!

---

[7] Keating recommends the repetition of a prayer word one chooses for themselves or with a spiritual director. This is a technique for quieting the mind known as "centering prayer." Other well regarded authors who wrote on this technique include Basil Pennington, a Trappist monk, and John Main, a Benedictine monk.

There are many helpful techniques for learning how to sit comfortably in silent prayer. We can't cover all of them here. A simple way for beginners is to focus on your breath coming in and out of your body. This also helps to relax us. Another method involves repeating a brief simple prayer, for example "Jesus, mercy." This is called the "Jesus Prayer." It is a shorter version of the prayer of the publican in Luke 19:9-14. "Lord Jesus Christ, Son of God, have mercy on me a sinner." It has been practiced by Christians around the world for over a thousand years. All those people can't be wrong!

Discursive prayer is how most people start a more serious prayer life. This can involve reading the Scriptures and meditating on them, reading a life of a saint and considering how to live and pray in light of his or her thought. One of the great holy men of our tradition, Brother Lawrence of the Resurrection, was a humble cellar monk, yet became famous for his holiness. His advice on prayer is simple yet powerful: practice the presence of God. He cooked and fetched and cleaned as part of his duties at the monastery. No matter what he did -- sweeping, shopping or shoveling -- he reminded himself of God's presence. Though he was a lowly monk rather than a priest in this monastery, people sought him out for advice because they felt God with him. All the others from his monastery are long forgotten, but Brother Lawrence is remembered to this day.

A classic teaching on prayer says: "Don't pray how you can't. Pray how you can." The technique is much less important than simply sitting down to give time to God. Trust in Jesus to guide you, and help you overcome all obstacles. He is faithful.

# APPENDIX C

# Saint Ignatius and "the Two Standards"

# App C: Saint Ignatius and "the Two Standards"

This famous spiritual exercise can help us choose light over darkness. It was composed by Saint Ignatius of Loyola, who lived in the 16th century and founded "the Society of Jesus," or the Jesuits.

Ignatius' early adulthood was spent as a courtier and adventurer. During a military battle he suffered a badly broken leg after being hit by a cannon ball. When he saw it was healing in an unattractive fashion, he ordered it re-broken and set again.

Recuperation required many months. During all that time in bed, he read and noticed something. If he had been reading adventure stories and romances, he would become interested but the excitement would fade and he subsequently found himself uninterested, dissatisfied and agitated. If he had been reading Scripture or the lives of saints, his interest continued, and he experienced peace and a desire to serve God. Something about placing himself before God had a lasting positive effect.

Ignatius eventually composed the *Spiritual Exercises* to help people more deeply appreciate the state of the world, the particularities of their own nature, and what God desires for one's life. "The Two Standards" is one of the exercises. Ignatius depicts the opposing forces of good and evil as armies, each gathered under its own flag, or "standard." The army of darkness and the army of light stand opposed on the field of battle.

## The Two Standards

Let's begin our prayer by placing ourselves in God's presence. Take a few deep breaths and remember that God is closer to us than we are to ourselves.

Ask God for the grace to focus on the movements of his Spirit during this exercise. Ask the Spirit to reveal your tendencies and previous choices when faced with making a decision between darkness and light.

Thank him for any blessings he will give you in this time.

Imagine Jesus Christ and His followers on a splendid green plain, with wonderfully colored pavilions and bright flags billowing in gentle breezes. Look across the field. Imagine the Satan with his followers in a deep ravine, all grays and shadows, and the air dead still.

Don't let this imaginary geography obscure the interior geography. It's our own hearts we are really exploring. Look there to learn where in you is darkness and where light. Ask yourself: "In what ways do I choose evil over good? "

Third, ask God to give you the courage to see clearly the face of good and the face of evil. Ask him to teach you to understand intimately the way the mind of Christ works. Also ask that he help you see the way people who have chosen the light make their decisions. Ask God what they value and how this guides their choices.

Next envision the commanders on both fields of battle. See a great field of the region of Jerusalem, where the supreme Commander-in-chief of the good is Christ our Lord. See also another field in the region of Babylon, where the chief of the enemy is Lucifer.

Ask for knowledge of the deceits of Lucifer, for Jesus calls him the Father of lies (John 8:44). Pray that you will be guarded against them. Ask for knowledge of the true life which the supreme and true Captain shows and the grace to imitate him.

Next imagine the chief of the enemy seated in that great field of Babylon, as in a great chair of fire and smoke, horrible and terrifying. Then consider how he issues a summons to innumerable demons in order to scatter them to do his work: some to one city and others to another, and so throughout the world, not omitting any countries, cities, or states.

## App C: Saint Ignatius and the Two Standards

Then consider how he instructs them, how he tells them to cast out nets and chains. Hear him encouraging his demons to first tempt with a longing for riches that men and women who gain them may more easily be pumped full of pride by nothing other than what they own, rather than who they are (vain honor). Next he tells them to tempt to vast pride. The first temptation is riches; the second, vain honor; and the third, pride. From these three vices men and women are drawn to all the rest.

Now turn to Christ's army. Consider how our Lord puts Himself in a great field of that region of Jerusalem, in a lowly place, beautiful and attractive.

Consider how the Lord of all the world chooses so many persons – apostles, disciples, etc., – and sends them through all the world spreading love and hope to every kind of person: married, single, rich, poor, old, young, laborer, executive.

Consider Christ our Lord instructing his servants and friends sent on this expedition, encouraging a desire to help all.

See the insults and contempt that the followers of our Lord encounter. From these humility follows. As with Lucifer's armies, there are three means of forming followers: the first, poverty against riches; the second, insults or contempt against worldly honor; the third, humility against pride. From these three come all the other virtues.

After you have imagined all these things, ask Our Lady to intercede for you. Ask Jesus, the Father and the Holy Spirit to help you learn whatever it is God has to teach you from this meditation.

Close with an Our Father and three Hail Marys.

# Small Group Discussion Guidelines

# Small Group Discussion Guidelines

A small Christian community seeks to foster a deeper and more meaningful connection with God and with one another. For many of you this will no doubt be a new experience. You may be wondering what will take place, will I fit in, and even will I want to come back? These are fair considerations. Here are some expectations and values to help clarify what this community will be about. Please read the following aloud and discuss if necessary:

## Purpose

We gather as Christians – our express purpose for being here is to explore together what it means to live the Gospel of Jesus Christ in and through the Church during the season of Lent.

## Priority

In order to reap the full fruits of this personal and communal journey, we will make participation in the weekly gatherings a priority.

## Participation

Each person has a unique relationship with God. We will strive to create an environment in which all are encouraged to share at their comfort level.

## Discussion Guidelines

The heart of our gathering time is our sharing in "Spirit-filled" discussion. This type of dialogue occurs when the presence of the Holy Spirit is welcomed and encouraged by the nature and tenor of the discussion. Will observe the following guidelines:

- Participants strive always to be respectful, humble, open, and honest in listening and sharing.

- Participants share on their level of personal comfort.

- As silence is a vital part of the total process, participants are given time to reflect before sharing begins.  Also, keep in mind that a period of comfortable silence often occurs between individual sharing.

- Participants are enthusiastically encouraged to share while, at the same time, exercising care to permit others (especially the quieter members) an opportunity to speak.  Each participant should aim to maintain a balance between participating without not dominating the conversation.

- Participants keep confidential anything of a personal nature that may have been shared in the group.

- Perhaps most importantly, participants should seek to cultivate a mindfulness of the Holy Spirit's desire to be present in the time spent together. When the conversation seems to need help, ask the Holy Spirit's intercession silently in your heart. When someone is speaking of something painful or difficult, pray the Holy Spirit to comfort them, as well as to aid the group to respond sensitively and lovingly. If someone isn't participating, praying for that person during silence may be more helpful than even a direct question. These are but a few examples of the ways each might personally invoke the Holy Spirit.

## Time

It is important that your group starts and ends on time.  Generally a group meets for about 90 minutes with an additional 30 minutes or so for refreshments.  Agree on these times as a group and work to honor them.

# The Role of a Facilitator

P erhaps no skill is more important to the success of a small group than the ability to facilitate a discussion according to the movement of the Holy Spirit. Such an approach recognizes the prominence of God's sanctifying Spirit in the spiritual journey, not necessarily our knowledge or theological acumen. The following guidelines can help facilitators avoid some of the common pitfalls of small group discussion, and open the door for the Spirit to take the lead in the "connection" we seek with Jesus Christ.

## You are a Facilitator, NOT a Teacher

It can be incredibly tempting to answer every question as a facilitator. Someone may have excellent answers and be excited about sharing them with their brothers and sisters in Christ. However, a more Socratic method, by which you attempt to draw answers from participants, is much more fruitful for everyone else and the facilitator.

Get in the habit of reflecting participants' questions to the whole group before offering your own input. It is not necessary for you as a facilitator to immediately enter into the discussion or offer a magisterial answer. When others have sufficiently addressed an issue, try to exercise restraint in your comments. Simply affirm what has been said, thank them, and move on.

If you don't know the answer to a given question, have a participant look it up in the *Catechism of the Catholic Church* and read it aloud to the group. If you cannot find an answer, ask someone to research the question and bring their discoveries to the next session. Never feel embarrassed to say, "I don't know." Simply acknowledge the quality of the question and offer to follow up with that person after some digging. Remember, you are a facilitator, not a teacher.

## Affirm and Encourage

We are more likely to repeat a behavior when it is openly encouraged. If you want to encourage more active participation and sharing, give positive affirmation to group members' responses. This is especially important if people are sharing from their heart. A simple "thank you for sharing that" can go a long way in encouraging further discussion in your small group.

If someone has offered a theologically questionable response, don't be nervous or combative. Wait until others have offered their input. It is very likely that someone will offer a more helpful response, after which you can affirm them by saying something like, "That is the typical Christian perspective on that topic. Thank you."

If no acceptable response is given, and you know the answer, exercise great care and respect in your comments so as not to appear smug or self-righteous. You might begin with something like, "Those are all interesting perspectives. What the Church has said about this is. . ."

## Avoid Unhelpful Tangents

There is nothing that can derail a Spirit-filled discussion more quickly than digressing into unnecessary tangents. Try to keep the session on track. If the group goes off on a tangent, ask yourself, "Is this a Spirit-guided tangent?" If not, bring the group back by asking a question that steers conversation to the Scripture or question you have been discussing. You may even suggest kindly, "Have we gotten a little off topic?" Most participants will respond positively and redirect according to your sensitive leading.

That being said, some tangents may be worth pursuing if you sense the action of the Spirit. It may be exactly where God wants to steer the discussion. You'll find that taking risks can yield some beautiful results.

## Fear NOT the Silence

Be okay with silence. Most people need a moment or two to muster up a response to a question. It is quite natural to need some time to formulate our thoughts and put them into words. Some may need a moment just to conjure up the courage to speak at all.

Regardless of the reason, do not be afraid of a brief moment of silence after asking a question. Let everyone in the group know early on that silence is an integral part of normal discussion, and that they shouldn't worry or be uncomfortable when it happens.

This applies to times of prayer as well. If no one shares or prays after a sufficient amount of time, just move on gracefully.

## The Power of Hospitality

It is amazing how far a little hospitality can go. Everybody likes to be cared for and this is especially true in a small group whose purpose it is to connect to Jesus Christ, our model for care, support, and compassion. Make a point to greet people personally when they first arrive. Ask them how their day was. Take some time to invest in the lives of your small group participants. Work at remembering each person's name. Help everyone feel comfortable and at home. Allow your small group to be an environment where authentic relationships take shape and blossom.

## Encourage Participation

Help everyone to get involved, especially those who are naturally less vocal or outgoing. A good way to encourage participation initially is to always invite various group members to read the selected readings aloud. Down the road, even after the majority of the group feels comfortable sharing, you will still have some quieter members who may not always volunteer a response to a question but would be happy to read.

## Meteorology?

Keep an eye on what we call the "Holy Spirit barometer." Is the discussion pleasing to the Holy Spirit? Is this conversation leading participants to a deeper personal connection to Jesus Christ? The intellectual aspects of our faith are certainly important to discuss, but conversation can sometimes degenerate into an unedifying showcase of intellect and ego. Discussion can sometimes take a negative turn and become a venue for gossip, complaining, or even slander. You can almost feel the

Holy Spirit leave the room when this happens! If you are aware that this dynamic has taken over a particular discussion, take a moment to pray quietly in your heart, asking the Holy Spirit to help you bring it back around. This can often be achieved simply by moving on to the next question.

## Pace

Generally, you want to pace the study to finish in the allotted time, but sometimes this may be impossible without sacrificing quality discussion. If you reach the end of your meeting and find you have only covered half the material, don't fret! This is often the result of lively Spirit-filled discussion and meaningful theological reflection. In this case you may want to take another meeting to cover the remainder of the material. If you only have a small portion left, you can ask participants to finish it on their own and to come to the following meeting with any questions or insights they have. Even if you have to skip a section to end on time, make sure you leave adequate time for prayer and to review the "Connecting to Christ This Week" section. This is vital in helping participants integrate their discoveries from the group into their daily lives.

## Joy

Remember that seeking the face of the Lord brings joy! There is nothing more fulfilling, more illuminating, and more beautiful than to foster a deep and enduring relationship with Jesus Christ. Embrace your participants and the entire spiritual journey with a spirit of joyful anticipation of what God wants to accomplish through your *CONNECTIONS* small group.

> These things I have spoken to you,
> that my joy may be in you,
> and that your joy may be full.
> John 15:11

# Materials to Have at your Small Group

# Materials to Have at Your Small Group

**Several materials may be very helpful to have on hand while facilitating your small group:**

## Bible

You and all members of the small group should bring a Bible to each session. It's a good idea to bring extras, if you can, for those who might forget. We recommend the *New American Bible,* the *Catholic Study Bible,* the *New Jerusalem Bible,* which has excellent footnotes, or the *Catholic Serendipity Bible,* which is not scholarly, but contains good devotional material.

## Catechism of the Catholic Church

Some sessions include reading selections from the *Catechism,* all of which are printed out in text for your convenience. However, you will want to have at least one *Catechism* at hand for referencing when questions come up in discussion. You might encourage all of your participants to purchase one for their own collection. It is an invaluable resource for private study and reflection.

## A Theological Dictionary

We recommend Image Book's *The Pocket Catholic Dictionary* by John A. Hardon, S.J. It offers concise definitions for a panoply of Catholic terms. As you are preparing for your small group, you may decide to make other materials available for purchase, such as some of the classic writings of the Catholic tradition. We have found this to be a great way to get good books into the hands of eager people.

# A Guide to the
Sacrament of Reconciliation

# *A Guide to the Sacrament of Reconciliation*

If it has been a long time since you last "went to confession," you may be hesitant and unsure. Join the club! Despite common fear and discomfort with this ancient practice of our Church, reconciling with God is always a cause of great joy in our lives. Take the plunge! You'll be glad you did.

Below is a step-by-step description of the process that may help alleviate your fears. No formula is as important as just being honest. Don't let concern about memorizing words and responses impede you from the freedom the scarament offers. If you don't remember what to say when, the priest will help you, usually graciously. You always have the option to go to confession privately behind a screen or face-to-face with the priest.

1. Prepare to receive the sacrament by praying and examining your conscience, perhaps with a tool such as the one included in the appendix of this booklet. If you don't like that one, many are available on-line. Search "examination of conscience" and you will find hundreds.
2. Begin by making the Sign of the Cross and greeting the priest by saying, "Bless me father, for I have sinned." Tell the priest how long it has been since your last confession.
3. Confess your sins to the priest. If you are unsure about something, ask him to help you. Place your trust in God, a merciful and loving father. When you are finished, indicate this by saying something like, "I am sorry for these and all of my sins."
4. The priest will assign you a penance such as prayer, Scripture reading or a work of mercy, service or sacrifice.
5. Express sorrow for your sins by saying an act of contrition such as the one below.
6. The priest, acting in the person of Christ, will absolve you from your sins by saying the "Prayer of Absolution," to which you respond by making the Sign of the Cross and saying, "Amen."
7. The priest will offer some proclamation of praise, such as "Give thanks to the Lord, for he is good," to which you respond, "His mercy endures forever."
8. The priest will dismiss you.
9. Go and complete your assigned penance.

## An Act of Contrition

O my God, I am heartily sorry for having offended you and I detest all my sins, not only because I dread the loss of heaven and pains of hell, but most of all because they offend you, my God, who are all good and deserving of all my love. I firmly resolve, with the help of your grace, to confess my sins, to do penance, and to amend my life. Amen.

# An Examination of Conscience

# An Examination of Conscience

**The examination may be considered silently as you prepare for your confession.**

Jesus said: "You shall love the Lord, your God, with all your heart, with all your soul, and with all your mind. This is the greatest commandment. The second is like it: You shall love your neighbor as yourself." – Mt 22:37-40

## Love is patient, love is kind. . .

- Do I love the Lord with all my heart, soul and mind, or do I hold back because of my love of possessions or status, or because of my own fears?

- Do I express my love for God with daily prayer and participation in the Mass? Do I express my patience and trust in the Lord by keeping Sunday as a holy day?

- Do I patiently wait for the Lord to hear my prayers, or do I take things into my own hands? Have I truly given the reigns of my life to God or am I trying to maintain control?

- Am I putting into practice those things God is calling me to do?

- Am I patient with my family, friends and co-workers?

- Do I treat others with true kindness? Am I generous with my time? Do I share my gifts with those in need?

- Am I true to my family relationships? To my friends? Do I act or speak one way in their presence and another when they are gone?

- Do I honor my parents and show them respect and love?

- Do I empathize with others, especially those who are poor and vulnerable or who seem difficult to love?

- Do I dishonor my body by fornication, impurity, unworthy conversation, lustful thoughts, evil desires or actions? Have I given in to sensuality? Have I indulged in reading, conversation, shows, and entertainment that offends Christian decency?

"[The sacrament of Reconciliation] is called the sacrament of conversion because it makes sacramentally present Jesus' call to conversion, the first step in returning to the Father from whom one has strayed by sin." –*CCC*, 1423

## Love is not jealous, it is not pompous, it is not inflated, it is not rude. . .

- Am I jealous of other people? Do I covet their popularity, wealth, possessions or abilities?

- Do I look down on others of different financial status, intelligence level, competence, or social class?

- Am I quick to judge others?

- Do I treat all people with respect and love?

- Do I interrupt people in conversation? Do my own thoughts, ideas and words take precedence over others'?

## Love does not seek its own interests, it is not quick-tempered, it does not brood over injury. . .

- Do I put aside my own wishes and desires to serve God, as well as my family, parish, and community?

- Do I become angry if things don't go "my way?"

- Am I quick to speak harshly to others? To strangers? To those I love?

## An Examination of Conscience

- Am I able to truly forgive others? Or do I hang onto pain and mistrust?

- Do I brood over wrongs others commit?

- Have I committed violence against others? Have I struck someone in anger? Am I abusive – physically or emotionally – of a spouse or child? Have I been involved with abortion?

- Have I stolen from someone or kept something that does not belong to me?

- Have I been faithful to my spouse?

- Have I had recourse to artificial contraception or sterilization?

**Love does not rejoice over wrongdoing but rejoices with the truth. . .**

- Do I rejoice in other's achievements or am I left threatened or defensive? Do I often highlight the negative in others' lives to make me feel better? Am I somehow pleased when others fail or are wronged?

- Do I expect the best or the worst from other people?

- Do I cherish the truth above all things or only when it is convenient or advantageous for me? Am I true to my own word?

- Do I gossip? Lie? Cheat?

"Whoever confesses his sins . . . is already working with God. God indicts your sins; if you also indict them, you are joined with God." -St. Augustine.

**Love bears all things, believes all things, hopes all things, endures all things. . .**

- Do I endure hardships in my life with patience, hope and joy in the Lord?

- Do I believe the tenants of the Catholic faith?

- Does my love of Christ compel me to live out the Church's beliefs in all facets of my life?

- Do I wait in joyful hope for our Lord's return in glory?

- Am I hopeful, even in the midst of the world's uncertainty?

- Do I try to manage the trials of my life on my own or by faith in God's goodness and provision? Am I willing to bear my own crosses as I follow in the footsteps of Jesus?

### A Prayer of the Penitent

Lord Jesus, you chose to be called the friend of sinners.

By your saving death and resurrection free me from my sins.

May your peace take root in my heart and bring forth a harvest

Of love, holiness, and truth. Amen.

*- from the Rite of Penance*

**the evangelical Catholic**
forming disciples. training leaders.

www.evangelicalcatholic.org

The following team created this study: Faye Darnall, Jason Simon, Mary Grace Simon, Sandra Kruse, and Brad Klingele. Thanks also to Eileen Hughes for helping to proof the manuscript.

Made in the USA
San Bernardino, CA
16 February 2015